ALSO BY
BARRY GLASSNER

BODIES: WHY WE LOOK THE WAY WE DO
(AND HOW WE FEEL ABOUT IT)

career crash

Barry Glassner

America's

New

Crisis—

and

Who

Survives

SIMON & SCHUSTER
NEW YORK LONDON TORONTO SYDNEY TOKYO SINGAPORE

SIMON & SCHUSTER
Rockefeller Center
1230 Avenue of the Americas
New York, New York 10020

Designed by Songhee Kim
Manufactured in the United States of America

1   3   5   7   9   10   8   6   4   2

Library of Congress Cataloging in Publication Data
Glassner, Barry.
Career crash / Barry Glassner.
p.   cm.
Includes index.
1. Career changes—United States. 2. Baby boom generation—
United States—Attitudes. 3. Middle aged persons—United
States—Psychology. 4. Job stress—United States. I. Title.
HF5384.G55   1994
650.14—dc20   93-32705
                                        CIP
ISBN: 0-671-69026-4

TO BETSY

A C K N O W L E D G M E N T S

For her extraordinary contributions as an editor and her willingness to stick with me through numerous revisions, I thank my wife, Betsy Amster. The book was also greatly improved by suggestions from Dominick Anfuso, my editor at Simon & Schuster. I appreciate the help Cassie Jones at Simon & Schuster provided as well.

My agent, Geri Thoma, has been a great advocate for the book as well as a good friend and wise critic. My colleagues at the University of Southern California and the University of Connecticut gave me the freedom and encouragement I needed throughout the entire five-year period in which I researched, wrote, and reworked this book. Valuable assistance with library research was provided by Marguerite Koster and Susan Aminoff, doctoral students at the University of Southern California.

Conversations with a great many people helped me in my thinking about careers, crashes, and the baby boom generation. In particular, I thank Charlotte Kahn, Ed Levine, Mauricio Mazon, Jonathan Moreno, Lillian Rubin, Morty

ACKNOWLEDGMENTS

Schapiro, Charles Smith, Barrie Thorne, Gaye Tuchman, and Syl Whitaker.

Above all, I am grateful to the baby boomers, career counselors, and therapists throughout the country who shared their time and their experiences with me.

C O N T E N T S

INTRODUCTION

This is about lucky people during a luckless period in their lives. It is about baby boomers, who have had more opportunities and advantages than any generation in American history. In particular, it is the story of those baby boomers with the *greatest* advantages—successful, college-educated boomers who, despite their good fortunes, crash out of their careers.

Some crash after receiving pink slips in the wake of massive layoffs in their industry. Paula Dunham* arrived one morning at the large insurance company in Hartford, Connecticut, where she had been working for fifteen years. On her desk was a note from her supervisor to see him immediately. "When he told me my job had been eliminated, my first reaction was that he must be joking," she recalled. "There had been several rounds of staff cuts, but I never believed it could happen to me. My performance reviews had always been excellent." Paula looked for another job, and when she couldn't find one, she felt so ashamed and dejected, for several weeks she rarely left her house.

*Her name, and those of all others whose personal stories I include, has been changed. In addition, certain identifying details and locations have been altered. Names of therapists, career counselors, and other professionals who are quoted for their expertise have not been changed.

Other baby boomers depart their jobs of their own accord. They suddenly realize they don't want to spend the second half of their lives doing work they dislike. To the everlasting shock of friends and colleagues, they simply walk away from positions that others in their profession would kill to have.

David Levin, an attorney, was in no danger of losing his job at the time of his career crash. True, the prestigious Wall Street law firm where he worked was behaving like many throughout the nation in the early 1990s and laying off every associate it could survive without. But David was widely regarded as a shoo-in for a partnership. His problem was that he felt trapped.

"I remember calling my wife on the phone and crying," said David. "I'd been working like a slave, eighty hours a week. I felt like I was in a submarine that was on fire, and somehow I had to get out." David spent a couple of weeks in bed and at doctors' offices with severe stomach cramps, and when they finally eased, he quit his job. No particular event had provoked David's crash, just an accumulation of evidence that, despite the big bucks he was making, he loathed the work.

By contrast, for Cal Wilson there was a very specific event that provoked his career crash—the death of his closest friend in a car accident. Following the funeral, Cal was unable to concentrate at his job as a land surveyor in northern California, and within a few weeks he quit.

After his friend died, Cal found himself plagued by memories from a traumatic period twenty years earlier. He had never let himself feel sorrow over the deaths of men he'd served with in Vietnam, and now he was overcome by pain and guilt.

On the day Cal left his job, he packed his car full of food and drove up into the mountains, where he camped out for the next five weeks. During that time he suffered horrible nightmares, cried a lot, and endured flashbacks to Vietnam whenever an airplane passed overhead. Several times he seriously considered suicide.

Fortunately, Cal made it through his ordeal, and afterward he and his wife set out to create a new life together. They moved to Los Angeles, where Cal got a job managing equipment for a film production company.

Career crashes do not necessarily have such happy endings, however, at least in the short run. Neither David Levin nor Paula Dunham have yet gotten back on track. A year after he quit the law firm, David is living mostly off his wife's income and trying to raise capital to start his own mail-order business. Paula, a single woman in her tenth month of unemployment, still vows she'll find another job in the insurance field, though so far she's had no luck.

In the rough-and-tumble economy of the 1990s, there's no telling when or where someone will land. After losing or leaving a job, you can reliably anticipate only one thing: the following year or two will not go quite the way you plan. People who get fired and put their houses on the market for fear of foreclosure secure new jobs the following week. And men and women who voluntarily resign from their jobs with definite arrangements for replacement positions wind up out of work.

When Francine Sundlan became aware that she was growing tired of nursing, she researched other types of jobs for which she might be qualified. Her tough times came not when she left the Minneapolis hospital where she had worked for ten years but a couple of months later. Immediately after she resigned, she enjoyed a sense of self-confidence and liberation she hadn't known since her teens. She'd gotten herself a choice job as manager of a research laboratory at a higher salary than what she'd been making. But a few weeks into her new job, her boss started coming on to her. By the end of her second month there, having figured out she wouldn't go to bed with him, he began to undermine her authority in the lab. Francine lost her self-assurance and sank into a depression.

• • •

Francine, David, Cal, and Paula are four among several hundred thousand baby boomers who have jumped or been pushed off career tracks on which they had expected to remain for life. As of mid-1993, approximately half a million boomer managers and professionals were out of work. At least as many more were expecting to leave their jobs soon, either because they hated them or because they anticipated losing them. No other generation of managers and professionals has experienced the same degree of job loss and disappointment since the Depression.

Career crashes have become a predictable crisis in many baby boomers' lives, as defining of their middle years as Vietnam or Watergate were for their youth. Rare is the baby boomer who will make it to age fifty without crashing. Even if he or she lucks out, the odds are excellent that a spouse, sibling, or close friend will not. A typical forty-year-old white-collar worker will change jobs two or three times before retirement, according to Drake Beam Morin, the nation's largest outplacement firm. The contrast to the previous generation, where people stayed with the same employer for life, could not be more acute.

This is the first book to examine in detail what happens to baby boomers before, while, and after their careers fall apart. It spells out the warning signs that precede a crash, the emotional reactions of depression, isolation, and self-doubt that inevitably accompany a crash, and the crucial stages involved in putting a career back on course.

Over a four-year period, I set out to discover why work has proven so problematic for this generation, and how baby boomers cope when their careers collapse. I collected information on career crashes suffered by nearly 400 baby boomers from all parts of the United States. I personally interviewed 120 women and men, about half of whom have gone through more than one crash. The remaining cases come from 60 helping professionals I interviewed—career counselors, psychologists, psychiatrists, and social workers from all regions of the country who discussed their case histories with me.*

The baby boomers in my study come from diverse professions—business, education, law, medicine, social services, engineering, public service, the arts. Their job titles ran the gamut of white-collar professional positions—manager, senior director, vice president, teacher, professor, nurse, physician, actor, producer, attorney, politician, agency head, engineer, systems analyst, writer, editor, creative director, stockbroker, banker, franchisee, independent entrepreneur.

For some of these people the cause of their career crash was obvious. They were laid off by their companies, or they got a new boss they despised so much they knew they had to leave.

But for others, the cause of their crash lay in their distant past. I met boomers who had betrayed their own true abilities and interests to pursue careers their parents wanted them to have, careers they grew to loathe during their thirties or early forties. And on the flip side of that coin, I met men and women who so resisted their parents' prodding that they became physicians' assistants instead of doctors, paralegals instead of lawyers, and missed their true calling.

Some crashes were provoked by the crashes of others. I spoke with boomers who, after surviving a couple of rounds of downsizing at their companies, bailed out before the ax could hit them, too. Within marriages, a surprising number of couples crashed serially. One partner quit or got fired, then within a few years, so did the other. "It was my turn," offered many married people in explanation. Cushioned by their spouses' income, the married people in my sample were likelier than the single people to see career change as a matter of entitlement.

• • •

*For details about the study, see "Methodology," pp. 199–200.

These are just some of the findings that emerged from my interviews with baby boomers. The chapters that follow are animated by their stories. Some are heartbreaking: I spoke with men and women who were fired or quit two or three years back and have scarcely begun to put their lives back together. But more often, these are hopeful tales. Most people I met are more content in their work lives today than they were before they crashed.

From their reports, a bigger picture emerges of how the baby-boom generation handles career crashes. That bigger picture can be useful to others in the same boat. People who are now in the throes of a career crash will find direction here as they ponder their options. (Do people like me benefit from career counseling? Should I consider going back to school for another degree? What can I tell the children?) So will those who expect to leave or lose their jobs in the future. (What are the signs that it's time to move on? How do people salvage their pride after being fired?)

My hope is that the stories that follow will help not only crashing baby boomers but also their wives, husbands, children, parents, and friends. Too often, these "significant others" make a difficult situation worse by pushing someone into a job that isn't really right for them, or panicking on their behalf. Knowledge of the predictable stages in a career crash can help allay anxieties and prevent permanent damage to relationships.

Many of the people in my study have devised resourceful routes back from their crashes. Instead of looking for the straight line they once followed, they have taken detours, backtracked, pursued parallel routes, and made forays into uncharted territory. In the end many have constructed enviable new lives for themselves at midlife. We can all learn from their example.

part
one

The

Workin

Wound

BOOMER BUST

Books, like people, change in the course of their development. This one started out to be about depression but ended up being about work.

Initially, my interest was sparked by a series of research reports that came out in the mid-1980s showing that a startling number of baby boomers were depressed. One study of almost 10,000 Americans, sponsored by the federal government, revealed that the rate of depression for people aged twenty-five through forty-four was about four times higher than for people over sixty-five. More than 8 percent of the baby boomers polled in another study had experienced an episode of major depression. Still other studies suggested that baby boomers have higher rates of depression than any other age group.

Until recently, it was the elderly, rather than younger adults, who had the blues. Before 1970, the older a person was, the less happiness he or she was likely to report in surveys. In the 1970s this trend disappeared, and it became impossible to pinpoint any statistical relationship between age and happiness. But during the 1980s, the earlier trend reversed itself. Now when people are asked to rank how happy they are, older Americans say they are happier than do people in their twenties, thirties, and forties.

Confronted by these surveys, I began to ask myself what made so many baby boomers so unhappy. Why was this generation suffering such malaise? Had baby boomers found adulthood too much to handle?

I went back and took a closer look at some of the surveys, and it was then that my attention shifted. Not all baby boomers are unhappy, of course, and those who *are* do not express dissatisfaction with every aspect of their lives. As a generation, boomers tend to be quite pleased with their friends and their health, for instance.

The major focus of baby boomers' discontent is their work lives. A recent Gallup poll discovered that people born after 1945 were far less pleased with their jobs than were older people. Nearly twice as many workers aged fifty or older said they were completely satisfied with their jobs than did younger workers, who were also less content with their chances for promotion and less likely to feel their skills were well utilized.

In explanation of the high incidence of depression in baby boomers, psychotherapists point to the perilously central role of work in the lives of men and women from this generation. Roberta Satow, Ph.D., a psychoanalyst in New York City, said of her clients, most of whom are women: "For many, their self-esteem is based on their careers. Their careers are really more primary than their relationships with men, in terms of their feelings about themselves. When these women begin to have doubts about their careers, their self-esteem takes a beating, and they become depressed."

Clara Waylee, Ph.D., a psychologist in Philadelphia who specializes in working with women managers and professionals, said much the same. Her clients tend to come to her in their thirties or forties after spending a decade or more building highly successful careers. "Then something goes wrong—they're hurt by the way they're treated by their industry, their marriage is falling apart—and it throws them," Waylee said. "They think this is not supposed to happen to them because they have put all their energies into their work and been so much in control their whole lives."

Male boomers, too, are showing up in large numbers at therapists' offices. In their case, the primary complaint is that the psychological dividends they anticipated from their careers have failed to materialize.

"They expected that work would solve their problems, that if they made it at work they would live happily ever after," said Nancy Fretta, who runs a depression clinic in Fairfield County near Washington, D.C. "One man in particular comes to mind. He did everything right, had his own law firm, and just couldn't be happy with it. He never really took time to decide what his priorities were. Once he made it financially and professionally and found he got no sense of satisfaction from that, it really sent him into a tailspin.

"He's like a lot of people we see who just got on the treadmill and kept going."

LESS THAN THEY HOPED

Throughout early adulthood, many boomers invested themselves in work to the virtual exclusion of everything else. The reason for this overinvolvement with work, according to a popular myth, is ingrained greediness. Pampered as children, baby boomers craved ever more and better playthings as adults.

For a small number of boomers, this explanation indeed applies. One thirty-five-year-old man I interviewed, a former commodities broker, admitted that he had been passionate about only one thing from childhood to the age of thirty-two—making money and spending it. He said he suspects he'd still be in that mind-set had he not been forced to recast his priorities after corporate downsizing eliminated his job.

Most boomers who fixated on their careers did so not primarily out of money lust, however. They did so by default. People in previous generations divided their loyalties among several social institutions—marriage, politics, religion, and work. But the first three of those lost their luster during the 1960s and 1970s, when most baby boomers were growing up. During those years, happily married couples were rarer than snowstorms in August, every politician boomers trusted was either assassinated or soundly defeated at the polls, and some of the best minds of the time broadcast the view that God was dead.

The state of the American economy also encouraged devotion to career. During the 1970s, while older baby boomers were establishing themselves in the work world and younger boomers were deciding what to do when they grew up, two major recessions took place, inflation was running in double digits, and mortgage rates reached 16½ percent. Then, in the 1980s, jobs began to evaporate. From Fortune 500 companies alone, at least three million jobs disappeared during that decade. At decade's end, the unemployment rate for managers stood at a thirty-year high.

Baby boomers realized that if they wanted to maintain the middle-class lifestyle their parents had achieved—if they hoped to hold on to the jobs they had and continue to pay off their loans—they had *better* dedicate themselves to their work.

But by the time the 1990s rolled around, large numbers of baby boomers had begun to notice something disturbing. After ten or twenty years of putting career first, they didn't have a lot to show for the effort. One quarter of college-educated baby boomers—more than twice as many as in the parents' generation—said they were dissatisfied with where they live. Some must reside, because of their jobs, in cities they dislike, and some can't afford the sort of housing they had been brought up to expect. Far fewer in this age group own their own homes than do people in their fifties and sixties, and fewer are homeowners in their middle years than were members of the previous generation when they were the same age.

Katy Butler, writing in *Mother Jones* magazine, told of some shocking statistics she and her husband pieced together during a visit to her parents' home. "My parents paid $190 a month—on a 5 percent mortgage—for a four-bedroom house on an acre of land in Connecticut. Bob and I, with a combined income slightly lower than my father's, paid $1,500 a month—on a 9 percent mortgage—for a five-room bungalow slightly larger than my parents' deck. Yet we felt lucky to afford a house at all," Butler wrote.

Upon her return to California, she got to thinking about her friends and *their* parents. "With few exceptions, most of their parents had cobbled together some version of the American dream: kids (the most expensive durable consumer good), education, houses, retirement accounts, and time to enjoy it all. My friends dressed and ate well, but most had only one or two elements of the dream we had laughed at in our twenties and now could not attain. We had to choose between kids, houses, and time."

Butler notes that baby boomers, widely considered incapable of deferring gratification, often have deferred what previous generations considered basic.

As for Butler herself, realizing she'd spent most of the decade of her thirties distraught and angry, she made a major decision. She quit her job to become a free-lance writer. "I decided that if the economy was going to deprive me of things I deeply wanted, it would not also take my time," she says. She traded in her career as a reporter and the regular paychecks and benefits that went along with it. To make ends meet, she buys beans instead of meat at the grocery store, and she goes to the library rather than the bookstore for reading matter.

Yet in her article Butler reports she no longer feels cheated. While she may not make much money, neither does she commute to a hectic office every day or eat Chinese take-out every night. And if she wants to reserve an afternoon midweek to spend with a friend, she can.

QUITTING TO SURVIVE

Other baby boomers crash out of their careers for precisely the reverse reason that Katy Butler did. Butler had a job doing something she likes—writing—but it did not pay enough to provide the lifestyle she thought her long hours entitled her to enjoy. Conversely, some people have jobs that pay more than enough to afford them houses, kids, and all the other components of the American dream but require them to do work they hate.

People in previous generations, if they made good money, perhaps paid less attention to whether their jobs were enjoyable. Those who grew up during the Great Depression, in particular, tend to rate their adult lives positively because they compare the present with a threadbare past. The surveys on happiness show that for people older than baby boomers, more money often equals more happiness, while among boomers, levels of happiness do not go up much as income rises.

David Levin, the lawyer who jumped off the partnership track at the Wall Street firm where he worked, expressed a sentiment frequently heard from many boomers. "I doubled my salary in three years, from a very high salary to an astronomical salary," he said, "but what good was it if I despised the practice of law?"

David admits he initially chose law "for the same reason as every other yuppie: the bucks." But at the same time, he honestly expected to enjoy the work. "I actually liked law school. I found it intellectually interesting and I liked working on *Law Review*."

Not long into his job at the firm, however, he grew frustrated, bored, and lonely. "A lot of law work is sitting with a pencil alone in your office or in the library," he said. "Here's a typical situation. You have a wonderfully creative meeting with clients from a company your firm represents. You and the other lawyers toss around ideas, then one of the clients stands up and goes like this"—David rubbed his hands together as if he was washing them—"which means they are going to leave the rest of the details to the lawyers to clean up.

"The clients go back to their companies, and we lawyers all go off into our separate offices and sit there until eleven o'clock at night, working on our separate pieces of the product that is deliverable the next morning."

David added, "You deal with the minutiae of documents, and I'm just not good at detail work unless I care about the larger picture. The thought of spending five minutes, let alone fifty hours, working on somebody's vacuum cleaner bag antitrust suit was enough to make me retch."

He stayed with the firm for five years, David explained, because he felt he had no choice. He couldn't figure out how he'd make enough money to pay the $3,500 per month in mortgage and co-op fees on his apartment overlooking Central Park.

Ultimately, it was David's wife, a graphic designer, who persuaded him to quit. Alarmed by the hundred-hour workweeks he had to put in and fed up with his constant bitching about his work, she suggested they live for a while on their savings and her salary, until David could find a new career option.

When David announced at the firm that he was quitting, he was stunned by the response he got. "I had a stream of associates come in and unburden themselves," he recalls. "The underlying theme was, 'I'm miserable and I wish I had the nerve to do what you're doing.'"

David had no idea so many of his colleagues were so unhappy, or that they would view his decision as brave. "It didn't seem courageous to me at all," David says. "It seemed like a simple act of survival. I was gobbling Tagamets against the ulcer I had developed; I had skin rashes the doctor said were caused by stress; and my marriage was in danger."

JUST ANOTHER MIDLIFE CRISIS?

David Levin, like most of the people I interviewed, had trouble attaching a name to what happened to him at his job. It wasn't "burnout," he rightly noted. Burnout happens to people who have been doing the same work for many years and have grown tired and apathetic, neither of which was true of David.

At one point in our discussion, David suggested that maybe he was going through a midlife crisis. "If I understand what a midlife crisis is, the touchstone is this notion that you're not going to achieve the goals you originally set out, and you realize the limitations of your life. Somewhere along the line I realized I wasn't going to make a million bucks, or if I did, I'd be miserable doing it."

At the same time, David was uncomfortable labeling his predicament a midlife crisis. "But maybe it's not really a midlife crisis, because I still have dreams and goals," he said. "If I'd stayed at the firm ten years longer it would have been a midlife crisis. I consider myself extremely lucky to have gotten out in my early thirties, before that could happen."

Many baby boomer crashes do occur considerably earlier than the traditional midlife crisis. But there are other, more fundamental differences between the career crashes the baby boom generation experiences and the midlife crises of people in the parents' generation.

People from the parents' generation settled into their adult lives in the 1950s and 1960s. Their numbers were small, the economy strong, and the sexual and divorce revolutions and Vietnam War were yet to come. Although major world and national events occurred, such as the Korean War and the Cuban missile crisis, people of that generation enjoyed relative personal stability during their twenties and thirties and had lots of reasons for optimism about their future. Men had been brought up to raise the standard of living for their families, women to care for home and children, and both were accomplishing their assigned goals.

Then came the 1960s and 1970s, and everything was turned upside down for this generation. A well-publicized "generation gap" came between them and their children. The civil rights and women's movements were transforming relationships between the races and sexes. And concurrent with all of those social changes, the "human potential movement" was under way, enjoining people to get in touch with their true feelings.

The familiar forms which this generation's "midlife crisis" took can be understood only in historically specific terms. Middle-aged men left their families in search of the sorts of spiritual and erotic fulfillment that the media told them others were achieving and they felt they had been denied. Similarly, the stereotypic female midlife crisis of that period—the "empty nest syndrome"—resulted when mothers were left behind in their suburban ranch houses while their daughters rushed out to embrace independent careers and sexual liberation.

The previous generation's midlife crisis was about lives that had come to feel barren, and its central theme was *death and decay*. Elliott Jaques, the psychoanalyst who coined the phrase "midlife crisis," postulated that what provokes such a crisis is a person's realization that he or she is mortal. Later psychologists who studied people during midlife crises have also noted that the hallmark of such a crisis is an acute sense of time running out. Indeed, a book directed at therapists goes so far as to recommend that those who treat patients in midlife should expect to find them suffering from "death anxiety" and exhibiting psychopathology as a result.

That may well have been good advice for therapists working with earlier generations. Men and women probably did start to worry about death at some point in their thirties and forties. After all, as recently as the early part of this century, half of all adults were dead by age forty-seven. But life expectancies have increased steadily throughout the twentieth century, and most baby boomers can expect to make it at least to their late seventies.

Although baby boomers may joke about their receding hairlines or sagging breasts, they don't see their physical demise as imminent. Nearly nine out of ten baby boomers rate themselves in excellent or good health. And in anticipation of a robust old age, baby boomers exercise, watch what they eat, and refrain from smoking.

Rather than *death* anxiety, baby boomers suffer from *life* anxiety. They see themselves living productively for a good forty or fifty more years and worry they will spend much of that time either in jobs they dislike or out of work entirely. Moreover, they find themselves in their middle years with lives that, far from feeling dull or empty, are overfull. During the decades of the 1970s and 1980s, the average American lost 37 percent of his or her leisure time, and the workweek increased from forty-one hours to about forty-seven hours. And baby boomers have the least free time of any group. Were they actually to devote as many hours each week as they'd like to their work, friends, lovers, children, and various athletic, artistic, political, and spiritual pursuits, they'd have none left for sleeping or eating.

Boomers feel overworked and despair that the situation will ever improve. With the mandatory retirement age abolished, the Social Security system running deficits, and boomers' own proclivity for spending rather than saving, who among them can expect to stop work and move to Florida in their later years the way some of their parents did?

CHARTING A NEW COURSE

The lives of baby boomers' parents evolved in a sequence of dependably ordered events. They dated during adolescence, married and started families and careers in their twenties, and then devoted themselves for the next twenty years or so to caring and providing for their children.

The previous generation's "life contours," as sociologist Neil Smelser has called them, were far more predictable. By the time boomers' parents reached midlife, they could make good sense of where they were in their lives and could realistically predict the future course their lives would take. In particular, professionals from the previous generation could reliably expect to gain more and more power, responsibility, and monetary rewards between their early twenties and mid-fifties, after which all of these would level off. Most of them expected their involvement in their profession to end abruptly with retirement at age sixty-five.

According to Smelser, a professional person's life could be expected to look like this:

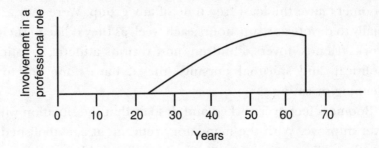

Baby boomers lead a much less well ordered existence. There is no blueprint for boomers' adult years. Some married in their twenties, others later, and about one in six will never marry at all. Among those who have children, some became parents for the first time in their early forties, while others at that age were already paying college tuition bills.

As for careers—compared to the calm drive through the countryside that the previous generation anticipated, the expected course of boomers' professional lives looks more like a rollercoaster ride. One reason is the economy: with all the corporate reorganizations and bankruptcies, recessions and recoveries taking place, baby boomers live in economically unstable times that preclude personal stability even for those who want it.

The other reason has more to do with the baby boom generation's values: boomers are too committed to change and experimentation to have steady, predictable careers during their middle and later years.

Unlike the previous generation, baby boomer professionals are destined to experience steep rises and falls over the course of their work lives: when they have children, or fall victim to retrenchment, or decide to test out alternative career or lifestyle possibilities.

I would graph the life contour of professional baby boomers this way:

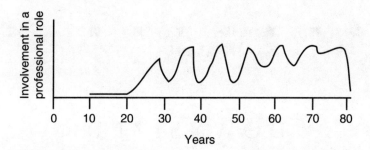

Exactly where the peaks and valleys come will vary from person to person. All one can say with certainty is that they will occur; baby boomers will have career crashes. A pressing matter at midlife is how to benefit from rather than be defeated by them. That is what this book is about.

DOWNSIZED
ACHIEVERS

Of the many routes to a career crash, the fastest and surest is to be fired. In the 1990s, with downsizing a routine part of American corporate life, it may also be the most common. During each of the last several years, between 36 and 56 percent of American companies cut their staffs.

Over the past decade, the number of unemployed managers and professionals has risen from about half a million to more than twice that number. One outplacement firm estimates that about 35 percent of middle-management jobs were eliminated between the early 1980s and the early 1990s. Management guru Peter Drucker anticipates that the situation will only get worse. By the year 2000, Drucker predicts, fully two thirds of the managerial positions that existed in the late 1980s will have been wiped out.

Until recently, managers in their thirties and early forties were virtually immune to layoffs. When companies tightened their belts, they squeezed out older workers and incompetents. But the average age at which managers are fired has been decreasing since the late 1980s. Baby boomers are now prime targets during downsizings.

Baby boomers may also have a particularly tough time finding new jobs. A survey of 250 managers who had been actively seeking new jobs for anywhere from six months to two years revealed that people in their mid-thirties to mid-fifties have the toughest time finding a new job. Only 55 percent of those surveyed had succeeded in that time frame, compared to 67 percent of managers who were either younger or older.

WHAT IT FEELS LIKE TO BE FIRED

The people I interviewed who lost their jobs said the experience was—at least early on—worse than they had feared. Quite apart from the turmoil of having to find another job, they were confronted with all sorts of unanticipated emotional reactions. First was the sheer shock of being out of work. Next came the hurt and anger at having been betrayed by their companies. Then there was the embarrassment of having to tell parents, partners, and children.

Cherished assumptions they held about themselves and the world suddenly were called into question.

"I'd never been involved in anything where I could be called a failure or less than extremely successful," said Paula Dunham, thirty-six, during our interview at her home in a suburb of Hartford, Connecticut, ten months after she was laid off from a job as a personnel manager in a large insurance company. "I was raised to believe that if you keep your nose clean and do a good job, you'll be rewarded. On some level, of course, I knew that wasn't really true anymore. In fact, I'd laid off people myself during earlier cutbacks. But knowing about it and going through it yourself are two different things."

It actually took about a month after she was fired before the cold reality of unemployment hit. Once she recovered from the initial jolt of being told by her supervisor, with no advance warning, that her job had been nixed, she hit the streets reasonably optimistic about her chances of finding another good position. She was an experienced human resources manager who knew a lot of people around town.

For the first several weeks, she was too busy making telephone calls and networking with friends over lunch or drinks to fret over her situation. And her efforts quickly turned up some promising leads, which renewed her faith that she'd be back at work before long.

The only actual job offers Paula got, however, were in the $25,000 range, half of what she had been making at the insurance company. By her fifth or sixth week out of work, she started to worry.

"I was doing everything I knew how to do," Paula recalled, "and it wasn't working." She found herself waking up mornings with nothing to do—no leads to pursue, no one left to call for lunch—and it drove her crazy. "I've always been a real workaholic, so twiddling my thumbs was torture. In my job I used to meet with thirty to forty people a day and probably again as many by phone. At home there was no one to talk to, the telephone never rang. I thought I would go stir-crazy. I'd turn on the radio and run the dishwasher just so there'd be some activity."

Because she was single, had some savings, and lived in a house she had bought a decade earlier with a small mortgage, Paula didn't have to worry she would go homeless. And although there were some weeks when her major source of protein was peanut butter, she knew she wouldn't starve.

On the other hand, the *meaning* of her lack of income began to upset Paula terribly. Although she would never call herself a feminist—there is a "Right to Life" sticker on the bumper of her aging Chrysler—her identity as a self-supporting career woman was crucial to her. The loss of that identity sent her into a tailspin.

Once her initial optimism faded, she became withdrawn. "I have always measured my worth by the fact that I can earn money," she said, "and the fact that I wasn't earning money made me feel like I didn't deserve things. I stopped going out to lunch, I stopped buying clothes, I canceled a vacation I'd planned to visit my sister in St. Louis. Every time I thought of doing something nice for myself, I'd stop myself. It was like, 'No no, you don't deserve that, because you don't have a job.' "

The three negative outcomes of being fired that almost no one avoids are depression, isolation, and self-blame. For close to a month, Paula suffered them all. She would oversleep at night, overeat during the day, and pass up opportunities to be with friends. Some days, she recalls, she wouldn't even answer the telephone. Instead, she stared at the TV, napped, and ate junk food.

"I was sinking into the typical housewife syndrome," she put it. "I had seen it with my mother after my sisters and I left home. Some of my friends who stay home with their children have gone through it, too. You turn into a soap opera addict."

But the worst part, Paula found, was how she blamed herself for losing her job. Objectively, she knew her performance had been excellent and that the only reason she was let go was that a company-wide reorganization had eliminated her job title. But none of that consoled her when she was unable to find another job.

"All I could think about was how I should have done things differently," she remembers. "I'd curse myself for not seeing the writing on the wall a year earlier and for every little mistake I'd made at work. I had myself convinced that if I'd been more conscientious, they would have considered me invaluable and protected me somehow."

THE TRAP OF SELF-BLAME

According to Hal Steiger, Ph.D., a psychologist in Minneapolis who specializes in treating victims of corporate downsizing, managers who are laid off chastise themselves mercilessly. "Even in companies that are downsizing by 30 percent," Steiger observes, "a lot of people will say, 'It's me, I'm a dummy, I wasn't savvy enough, I didn't position myself well, I should have known better.'"

Such self-blame inevitably exacerbates depression. "A sure way to stay depressed is to assume that you have control over things over which you have no control," Steiger notes.

By the same token, self-blame is something of an occupational hazard among managers. The very definition of a good manager is someone who assumes responsibility and takes control, who is unambiguously "in the driver's seat."

Katherine Newman, an anthropologist at Columbia University who studied unemployed managers, has argued that inappropriate self-blame is merely the flip side of one of the most widely held tenets of American corporate culture—that people succeed because of their own hard work. "When the successful fall from grace," Newman has written, "this ideology boomerangs. For if individuals are responsible for their own destinies, there is no one else to blame in case of failure."

Some people never break out of their cycle of self-blame, depression, and isolation, Newman found. In her book *Falling from Grace*, she describes several managers who went to pieces after losing their jobs. They became embittered, stopped taking care of themselves, started drinking, and gradually lost contact with friends and family. Some even committed suicide.

Fortunately, such dire outcomes are rare. Most professionals pull themselves together and make a concerted effort to get on a career track again. Accustomed to being active, directed people their entire lives, they quickly tire of wallowing in despair and develop a game plan for getting themselves reemployed.

Most people pursue one of two very different approaches. Either they tirelessly search out a job similar to the one they lost or else they treat their unemployment as a blessing in disguise and chuck their old career in search of a new one.

Ralph Turner, a professor of sociology at UCLA, has pointed out that most people think about themselves and their problems either "institutionally" or "impulsively." Those who think about themselves institutionally focus on the roles they occupy, with career and family roles first. By contrast, those who think about themselves impulsively concentrate on their true likes, dislikes, and desires, quite apart from whatever roles they may have.

A person recovering from a job loss can take one or the other approach. She can set out to recover her institutional self by replacing the career role that was lost. Or she can give a hearing to her impulsive self by asking what she *really* wants, independent of her previous job.

Which of the two strategies people gravitate toward depends largely on what sort of control they seek. Anyone who has been fired is likely to harbor a desperate desire to feel in control. But different people seek different sorts of control. Some desperately want to regain the sense of competence and authority they enjoyed before they were fired and so seek another job like their last. Others never honestly felt in control in their previous jobs in the first place. They didn't like the work they were assigned or felt their skills weren't put to good use, and so they seek a new career opportunity where they can have more of the kind of control they lacked in the past.

THE ROAD BACK

Paula Dunham is among those who have chosen the institutional route. She methodically searches for a job that would give her her old work role back, or one very much like it.

She remembers how, after three weeks of despair, she looked in the mirror and said, "You look awful. Get yourself together. You're a capable manager—go get yourself a job." She cleared out the spare bedroom that same morning and went to the store and bought a couple of gallons of paint.

Within a week Paula had turned the spare room into an office right out of *Working Woman*. Painted a bright off-white and equipped with a computer borrowed from a friend, an oak desk she bought at a house sale and refinished, and a rocking chair that has been passed down in her family, the office is far nicer than the drab one she occupied at the insurance company.

Although she is still out of work, Paula, too, looks more like a model in a magazine for executive women than someone who has been on the dole for almost a year. She has long since lost the weight she put on when she was depressed, and for our interview she wore one of two outfits she bought at Ann Taylor (on sale, but up-to-date) for business lunches and interviews.

Paula described the daily routine she has imposed on herself, a routine more rigorously scheduled and demanding than that of most employed people. She is out of bed by seven-fifteen, runs four miles, showers, eats breakfast, and is at her desk by nine. Weekday mornings she spends on what she calls her "merciless mailings." At latest count she had sent out eight hundred letters, each personalized by means of the "mail merge" function on her word-processing program. With every letter she encloses one of seven different résumés she has prepared to position herself properly for whatever job in the human resources field she applies for.

Most of her mailings have gone to headhunters she selected from the *Directory of Executive Recruiters* or to advertisers in *The National Business Employment Weekly*. But she tries more creative strategies as well. On her desk the day I visited were pages she had Xeroxed at the library from a book on the best companies in America for women. Paula had written down the names and addresses of the CEOs for thirty of these companies and was in the process of writing to each of them. Her hope was that at least a few of their secretaries would be sufficiently impressed by her cover letter to pass her materials along to their bosses.

Paula ends her mailing operation by noon each day and makes herself a sandwich or drives downtown to meet a friend for lunch. By two o'clock she is back at work. Most afternoons she spends answering the occasional serious inquiry—there have been about thirty thus far—that comes in response to her mailings. Or else she spends time at the library or on the telephone digging up new leads.

Where does someone find the wherewithal to maintain such discipline week after week in search of a job? It typically takes a woman manager 38 percent longer than a man to find new employment, according to a recent survey. And when she succeeds in finding a job, very likely it will be at a lower salary than her previous one. One major outplacement firm discovered in a survey of its clients that 40 percent accepted reduced incomes.

Personality certainly plays a role. Those who were highly organized and able to handle rejection prior to a career crash are most likely to be able to draw on those same skills afterward.

But something else is true of Paula and other baby boomers who doggedly pursue leads back into their old careers: this is not the first time in their lives they have had to deal with a serious disappointment or loss. Those as resilient as Paula have learned from a previous experience—the death of a loved one, a failed relationship—the importance of maintaining dignity and resolve in the face of adversity. Instead of viewing their present predicament as unique and overwhelming, they fit it into a larger picture of who they are and how they want to be perceived.

During our interview, Paula Dunham referred several times to her marriage and to the divorce that ended it a half-dozen years earlier. At first I thought she was trying to avoid my questions about her current difficulties. But gradually I came to appreciate how her struggles during and after her divorce gave her the ability to remain so resolute in her job quest.

Paula's marriage was a disaster from the start. Her husband had been a heavy drinker while they were dating in college, but she had attributed his behavior to the fact that he belonged to a fraternity. In the early years of their marriage, Paula denied her husband's alcoholism every bit as strongly as he did himself. She would make excuses when he got drunk at family barbecues, and when his drinking caused him to lose his job, she became the major breadwinner.

Paula says she still isn't certain how she finally found the courage, six years into the marriage, to leave her husband, after he dropped out of Alcoholics Anonymous for the third time. But she's very clear about the lessons she learned in what turned out to be a long and nasty divorce battle.

For one thing, Paula vowed never again to commit herself to something or someone just for the sake of being settled. She was the last of three sisters to marry, and being the oldest, she had begun to worry that she never would. So when her husband-to-be proposed to her, she accepted in spite of reservations she had about him.

She says she learned from that mistake to look closely before leaping into major commitments, whether in relationships or jobs. She also learned from her marriage—or rather, her divorce—how to fight for what she deserves, and how to live decently until she gets it.

When Paula left her husband and filed for divorce, her life seemed to go from bad to worse. She was the first person in her conservative New England family to divorce. Upon hearing that her husband would not move out of the house and was resisting the divorce, her parents and sisters urged her to reconcile with him. Instead, Paula rented a tiny apartment, hired a lawyer, and fought her husband in court for over a year. In the final settlement, she had to pay him half the market value of the house, even though she had made most of the mortgage payments while they were married. But she felt victorious at having stuck to her guns and gotten her house back.

On the other hand, by the time Paula moved back in, she was in debt from the legal costs and the house was a shambles. "It was early fall, and I just sat down in the backyard and cried," Paula remembers. "There were so many leaves to be raked, and the grass hadn't been mowed in months. It was overwhelming, and I didn't have any money to hire people to help.

"But I wasn't going to have the neighbors thinking, 'That house is a wreck; it's because a single woman lives there.' I borrowed a mower and a rake from a friend and just kept going until I got it done."

In the months that followed Paula devoted every weekend to a home repair or improvement project. She reglazed the storm windows, insulated the attic, retiled the bath.

Always disciplined, Paula became all the more so as she struggled to put her home back together after her divorce. And likewise in her current predicament, she dedicates herself to putting her career back on line.

It is hard to imagine anything that would divert Paula from her quest. "I'm going to get back into my field or die trying," she said to me, and I believe her.

A BLESSING IN DISGUISE?

Not everyone who initially takes the institutional route after a job loss continues down that path. Some end up making impulsive career moves. An investment banker I met in New York described how his priorities shifted radically when he lost his job. "In the past, I probably defined my self-worth about 90 percent in terms of my job title and how big and powerful I was. Now those things don't enter into my image of myself at all," said Harris Fullerton, forty-four, a Wharton MBA who worked for fifteen years on Wall Street and is now a free-lance financial consultant. A few years ago, when he was pulling in a quarter of a million dollars a year, "the most important things were the Mercedes and the summer house." Today, some years after he was laid off, he says his main interests are "putting greater meaning into life and spending time with my wife and daughter."

Outplacement counselors like to say that a layoff can be a stroke of good fortune for some people. "I don't look at downsizing as a catastrophe, I look at it as an opportunity," they say. "It's a chance to reassess your goals and values."

Such claims obviously smack of professional rationalization. Most outplacement counselors are employed by corporations to make ex-employees feel better about what's been done to them. They can hardly tell their "clients" the truth—that for most people most of the time, losing a job is a major setback.

For one group of boomer professionals, however, layoff notices truly *can* be heaven-sent tickets to personal growth. These are people like Harris, who otherwise would not step far enough outside their daily routines to see that they no longer want them.

The way Harris conducts his life has changed radically over the past couple of years. Where he used to get into his office at dawn to call Europe and stay late to call the West Coast and Japan, these days he walks his eight-year-old daughter to school almost every morning. More often than not, he picks her up afterward as well.

The last time Harris set foot on Wall Street was to buy a camera at one of the many discount stores near there. On the rare occasions when he walks into an office building, it's hardly ever into a gleaming skyscraper. As an independent consultant to nonprofit organizations, he works mostly in the rather humble spaces provided by the foundations, colleges, and arts organizations that contract with him or in the office he set up at home.

Over lunch at a Greek coffee shop not far from his co-op apartment on Manhattan's Upper West Side, Harris told me the story of someone who first responded to being fired by trying to find something like his old position but had then experienced a kind of spiritual awakening and decided to forsake his previous career to search for something more meaningful.

Harris was fired in 1990, during one of the many waves of layoffs that put about 69,000 securities-industry employees out of work in the first three years after the 1987 stock-market crash. His immediate reaction was panic. He took advantage of the office and secretary the firm offered him, seeking out other investment banking jobs on Wall Street.

"You can be very rigid about how you think about the world and your possibilities when you have a family and a big mortgage," he explained, sounding almost apologetic about his earlier behavior. "Even a major dislocation like being fired isn't enough to throw you off the path you've been charging down for fifteen years."

Despite the poor economic climate, within a couple of months he located several job possibilities and was actually in the process of accepting an offer when two tragedies permanently changed his outlook. First, his daughter was mugged and beaten while walking to visit a friend a few blocks from home. Harris spent every night over the next several weeks by her bedside, first at the hospital and then at home.

"Somehow having to deal with something like that, you put other aspects of your life in a different perspective," said Harris. "Being with my daughter took on a higher order of significance for me than my anxiety about being out of work. In a strange way, it calmed me down and helped me get my priorities straight."

The other tragedy that confronted Harris during that same period was the suicide of a former colleague, an executive at a major bank who jumped out the window of his penthouse apartment. He had lost his job right after the market crashed, and although he found another position two months later, he was never the same. At the funeral, a mutual friend told Harris that the man had been haunted by the fear of losing his new job and winding up destitute. Rather than waiting for fate to push him out onto the streets, he did it himself.

BREAKING THE MOLD

"When I was first laid off, all I focused on was regaining the security of a job, but there isn't any real security," Harris told me. "A lot of people believe that if you keep on doing a good job, everything is going to be fine.

"That philosophy may have worked in my father's day," he went on, "but not today. The world has changed. Too many companies are going through retrenchments and reorganizations. The only real security today comes from within."

Some people, having come to such a realization, would sign up for meditation classes or enter psychoanalysis. Harris turned for help to an organization called Crystal-Barkley, a career-consulting company in Manhattan. With money from his severance funds, he paid them $1,430 for an intensive five-day workshop plus five hours of personal consultations with their career counselors.

Based on the methods of John C. Crystal, a flamboyant former spy whose ideas formed the basis for Richard Bolles's best-seller *What Color Is Your Parachute?*, the Crystal-Barkley workshops devote relatively little time to the nuts and bolts of looking for a job, such as writing a résumé or surviving a job interview.

Instead, the focus is on helping people identify what they want from work and break out of the institutional mode long enough to get it. As Joseph Wiseman, a vice president at Crystal-Barkley, explained to me, most people believe they can only get jobs for which they have had formal training or experience. "But what we find is that most people have a wealth of transferable skills. They can learn how to adjust to new situations and be successful in them. They can go into almost any field or specialty they choose and do very well at it," Wiseman said.

Participants in Crystal-Barkley workshops spend many hours writing and analyzing their "life stories." With the help of workshop leaders, they reevaluate important events from their childhood and early adult years to ferret out their true passions and favorite skills.

For someone who has been on a straight-and-narrow career path, the experience can be enlightening. Harris Fullerton, for instance, had never asked himself what he would like in a career. The oldest son of a CEO at a Fortune 500 company, Harris had been en route to a business career since kindergarten. In college he majored in business and immediately afterward went to Wharton, where, as he remembers, "the best and the brightest were going into investment banking, and being reasonably competitive, I wanted to see if I could run with the crowd."

Harris was asked during one of the Crystal-Barkley sessions to close his eyes and visualize the ideal work environment. He came up with a big room filled with five desks. The implication was clear: the more projects Harris could juggle, the happier he'd be. By the time he left the workshop, he had decided to go out on his own and develop some of the business plans he had thought of but had never been able to pursue on Wall Street.

It was eye-opening for Harris to discover some themes in his own biography that suggested he might have pursued a very different career path from the one he'd taken. "It goes back to how I played with my Erector Set when I was four," Harris reported, slightly abashed. "I didn't just make a house or tower or something, I made four or five things at the same time. As ludicrous as it sounds, I think that's the key to why I was always bored at the firm and would initiate new projects of my own when I should have been concentrating on the project I was assigned."

His first move was to borrow several financial and desktop publishing programs from friends. Using the personal computer his old firm had bought him a couple of years earlier, Harris developed capitalization plans and prepared handsome-looking business proposals. Then he networked his way around town, pitching his ideas to decision makers in corporations and banks. Harris's most ambitious idea was to franchise a new concept in programming to cable television companies—local MTV-style shows. Using radio personalities from FM stations as hosts and videos by both national and regional bands, a cable company could essentially create the television equivalent of a hometown radio station. One of Harris's buddies from Wharton, now a cable TV tycoon, thought the idea had promise.

The only problem was, no one was buying. A year prior to our interview, after twelve months of hard work, not one of his ideas looked like it would fly, and Harris began to worry.

He hit upon independent financial consulting almost by accident while researching another new business idea that refused to take off. The idea had been to exploit the housing bust in the Northeast of the early 1990s. Construction companies were desperate for work, and Harris figured he could persuade them to shave prices or accept deferred payments. He set out to identify colleges in upstate New York where off-campus housing for students was in short supply and where he could locate wealthy alumni who would form real estate limited partnerships with him for sentimental and tax reasons.

During a fact-finding trip he met with the alumni director at one of the colleges. The man was discouraging about the prospects for Harris's housing plan, but at the end of their meeting he complimented Harris for the professionalism of his presentation. Too bad Harris wasn't on the job market, the alumni director said, because they could use somebody like him for a fund-raising campaign they were about to start.

"Presto! I turned myself into a financial consultant," Harris told me with a laugh. "I indicated that I was available on a contract basis for that sort of work." The alumni director immediately called the secretary to the president of the college and set an appointment for the two of them to interview Harris for the job.

"The president's first question," Harris remembers, "was what experience I had with college fund-raising. And I said, 'Absolutely none. But you are looking for a fresh perspective and problem-solving skills, and I have both in abundance. I can do something for you here.'"

For Harris, the ability to shift gears and sell himself that day meant the beginning of a new career. There were some rough weeks early on in his work with the college—the staff in the Alumni Development Office resented his presence, and the college president rejected all of his early suggestions—but his initial three-month contract was renewed. And in the course of meeting with members of the college's Alumni Association, he got himself into a new "loop," which resulted in consulting jobs with other nonprofit groups.

Harris doubts he will ever again make the huge sums he brought in as a Wall Street investment banker in the Roaring Eighties. But when three o'clock rolled around and he ended our interview to walk his daughter home from school, it was obvious he didn't care.

CHAPTER 3

THE CAREER
DIVORCE

"**I**f the office in which I toil has anything in common with a million other offices in this county, if friends of mine in various fields are a barometer of what our thirtysomething brothers and sisters throughout America are thinking, it appears that we've about reached the end of our respective ropes," wrote Peter Ivan Hoffman, a communications firm executive, in an op ed article in *The New York Times* in 1990. "All I hear these days is, 'I've got to do something else.' Or, 'I've got to change my life,' or 'There's gotta be something better.' These are not the usual sighs after a tough day. These are the words of people in real self-doubt; the words of those who are seeing the best years of their lives slip into the corporate black hole to support the life style they've bought into."

Hoffman dubbed the 1990s the "Flee Decade." Even as many baby boomers are forced out of their jobs, many others leave voluntarily. Rather than sink farther into "the black hole," they quit and seek other ways to support themselves.

Few of their parents would ever have done such a thing. To

walk away from a career, especially one that required an advanced education and paid reasonably well, was taboo until very recently. In the mid-1970s, when the psychologist Seymour Sarason wrote his book *Work, Aging and Social Change,* people still subscribed to what Sarason called "the one life–one career imperative." You chose your career when you were young and stayed in it until retirement.

After World War II, when baby boomers' fathers embarked on their careers, they had one goal in mind: to get back what the war had taken away from them. They hungered for security, prosperity, and respectability, and if their jobs provided at least a modicum of each, they stuck with them until retirement.

Tom Rath, the central character in the 1955 bestseller *The Man in the Gray Flannel Suit,* is the prototype for that generation. In the several years after the war ended, Tom and his wife produced three children and set out to acquire the requisites of a proper postwar suburban lifestyle—"a big house and a new car and trips to Florida in the winter, and plenty of life insurance."

They soon got all of that and more, thanks to the managerial position Tom landed at a public relations firm in Manhattan. Tom's reaction to the day-to-day demands of his job was not so different from baby boomers' job-related complaints today: he distrusted his boss, longed for more meaningful work, resented having to miss dinner with his family to attend evening meetings, and worried about becoming just another of the "bright young men in gray flannel suits rushing around New York in a frantic parade to nowhere." At one point, his disaffection with his work grew so great that he started drinking and abusing his wife and kids.

Still, Tom never quit. Instead, as he progressed through his thirties in the course of the novel, he adopted a philosophy of life—one characteristic of his generation—that practically guaranteed he would stay in his corporate job until retirement. "Money is the root of all order," he postulated one morning on the train ride from Greenwich, Connecticut, to Grand Central Station, "for one doesn't bring up children in an orderly way without money, and one doesn't even have one's meals in an orderly way, or dress in an orderly way, or think in an orderly way without money."

But the children of Tom Rath's generation are often unwilling to put up with jobs for the sake of the money. When career counselors ask their baby boomer clients to prioritize what they want from a job—money, prestige, flexibility, meaningful work—money does not come out on top. Meaningful work and flexibility do.

While baby boomers may be no less *fond* of money than their parents, they enjoy it for the material comforts it affords, not because they believe money will bring order to their lives. Boomers haven't lived through a period of outright economic collapse like the Great Depression, nor were their early careers preempted by a world war. So they do not share their parents' fears of being permanently without a good income or exalted title.

Nor do baby boomers share their sense of obligation to a profession. In 1977 Seymour Sarason noted that "our society has made it easier to change marriage partners than to change careers." At that time, with psychologists advocating divorce as a healthy alternative to an unsatisfying marriage, and divorce rates steadily climbing, people felt almost *encouraged* to leave bad marriages. By contrast, the "one life—one career imperative" dictated that they stick with their careers through thick and thin.

Now the pendulum has swung in the opposite direction. People who commit to marriages are hesitant to abandon them if they go sour. Before filing for divorce, they will go for marriage counseling, make radical changes in their personal habits, even move to a new city to accommodate their spouse. But if they find themselves in a bad work situation, they feel justified in simply leaving.

Baby boomers talk about quitting a career in the same ways that people their age a couple of decades ago spoke about ending a marriage. If you got into the wrong career when you were young, admit your mistake and get out. If the passion is gone from your career, locate a new one that turns you on. If your boss forces you to live in a city you hate, find a new employer in a place you like.

In part, these attitudes are a response to recent upheavals in corporate America. In much the same way the sexual revolution of the 1960s and 1970s weakened marital ties, the downsizing revolution of the 1980s and 1990s has weakened work ties. In the past, people felt a moral obligation to be loyal to their companies, who were loyal to them—a notion that has become quaint amid all the promiscuous layoffs and restructurings companies engage in.

"By breaking the lifetime-employment contract, companies substituted not a new contract, but a sort of threat. It was: We can fire you at any time, for any reason," noted Amanda Bennett, a writer for the *The Wall Street Journal* in *The Death of Organization Man*. The managers and executives Bennett interviewed, most of whom were in their fifties and sixties, had redirected their energies away from corporations and into other activities such as sports, volunteer work, and religion. "As work became more tumultuous, less understandable, more unpredictable, and less satisfying, many turned to outside interests," Bennett reported.

Among baby boomers, who are younger, an even more radical shift is taking place. Rather than augmenting their work lives with other activities, some boomers leave their companies entirely. They abandon big corporations in favor of smaller firms or businesses of their own, where they have greater control over their time and the work they're called upon to do.

BAILING OUT

One evening a couple of years ago, Craig and Libby Mullen made a fateful decision at supper. Sitting around a crowded kitchen table in their Manhattan apartment with their three young sons, they resolved to move to the country.

It was a dream Libby and Craig had discussed time and again throughout the ten years they'd been together. This time they set a definite date. Within the next three months, Craig would quit his job as circulation director at the magazine where he had worked for eight years, Libby would notify their landlord that they were not renewing their lease, and the entire family would abandon the big city for good.

Several factors motivated the Mullens to act when they did. One was the ages of their children. For their five-year-old son they were about to be forced to choose between a financially strapped public elementary school or one of several private schools whose tuition bills they couldn't afford. And for their active three-year-old twin boys, they wanted play space.

Libby and Craig believed *themselves* to be at a critical age as well—"the juncture of now or never, where either you make a change very soon or you never will," as Libby put it.

Libby, who was thirty-five at the time, wanted to resume the free-lance writing career she had put aside when the twins were born. "Craig and I went into this marriage intending to be equal partners and parents, but his job involved more and more travel, and I became a full-time mom," Libby explained during one of several conversations we had over the eighteen-month period following their decision to move. "We didn't want our sons growing up with a professionally unfulfilled mother and a father they saw only on weekends, so we decided to forcibly alter the situation."

After Craig found a job at a magazine in Charlottesville, Virginia, the family bought a gentrified farmhouse just outside of town. For the first few months after they moved there, all five of them were delighted with their choice. With the new swing set, sandbox, and puppy their parents bought them, the three boys had no complaints. Libby, sequestered four to six hours every day in her air-conditioned attic office, got plenty of writing done. As for Craig, he suddenly had time to play basketball and refinish furniture, favorite activities for which he'd had no time in recent years.

Although Craig took a 45 percent salary cut, he had no regrets. "A lot of guys get fixed onto one track and can't get off, and I didn't want that to happen to me," said Craig, who turned forty the same month they moved. "It's very enticing to just coast along once you're paid well and you can do the job on automatic pilot. But it's important to tear yourself away from that and really examine whether you have a life."

NO EASY SOLUTIONS

For Craig and Libby, as for so many people who trade in their old lives for new, the euphoria of escape lasted only a couple of months before unanticipated problems intruded. "I had expected my job to be easy, a scaled-down version of what I had before," Craig explained, "but it wasn't. There was no travel and no breakfast and dinner meetings like in New York, and that was nice. But in a small company you have to be a jack-of-all-trades. You have to do tasks yourself that at a bigger company there would be whole other departments for."

Craig discovered he had little aptitude for some of the new skills expected of him, such as designing subscription solicitations. To make matters worse, his management style conflicted with his boss's. His boss insisted on loads of meetings, which Craig considered a waste of time, and he delegated almost no decision-making authority to him, which Craig found insulting.

"I'd lie awake at night cursing him for being so rigid, and

cursing *myself* for being such a dummy that I couldn't learn what I needed to do the job right. I also worried about how my family would survive if I lost this job. There isn't another magazine of any size within a hundred and fifty miles."

By his fifth month there, Craig's unhappiness spilled over into his relationships at home. He was short-tempered with the kids, and toward Libby he became downright hostile. "I accused her of forcing me into this move," he recalled, "which was very dishonest, since I had wanted it as much as she had. I guess I had to have somewhere to let out my frustrations."

When one day Craig returned home from the office with the news that he had been asked to interview for an executive position by a national magazine headquartered on Long Island, Libby wasn't sure whether to cheer or cry. For the first time in months, Craig looked happy, but the last thing she herself wanted to do was move back to the New York area.

"My secret hope," Libby said, "was that he would miss the beauty of our mountain paradise and remember how horrible it was to work in a big company. Then maybe he'd come home and find some way to make peace with his job."

On the contrary, when Craig returned to Charlottesville—job offer in hand—all he could talk about was how exciting it would be to "play in the big leagues again." Armed with brochures from the local chamber of commerce extolling the fine schools and safe neighborhoods in the town where his new company was located, he immediately set out to persuade Libby that the whole family would enjoy it there.

"My heart sank," Libby recalled a couple of weeks later. "I was totally powerless. I really like it in Charlottesville, and I feel like we're going backward instead of forward. I'll be playing Donna Reed at home again, only in an ugly suburb instead of the city. But if I refuse to move, Craig will never forgive me."

Sooner or later they would have to move anyway, Libby figured, because Craig could not remain indefinitely in a job he hated. So the agreement the two of them worked out was for Craig to go to Long Island alone for a couple of months until the school year ended, when Libby and the kids would join him.

THE ROLLER-COASTER RIDE

People who heroically chuck their jobs and start anew often find that utopia is not around the corner, where they imagined it to be.

Frequently they have to go through hell. Subsequent jobs turn out worse than the ones they left, relationships become strained, savings are squandered.

The Mullens' experience is the rule rather than the exception—and their roller-coaster ride did not end once Craig took his new job. When I checked in on them midsummer, they were still living in Charlottesville. Libby and the three boys never *did* move back up north. Instead, Craig had quit his job three weeks after he started.

"When the owner of the company sat me down and explained the system they used to fudge circulation figures, I knew I wasn't going to be comfortable there," Craig explained. Shaken and depressed, he returned to Charlottesville, and by the time I saw him, nearly twelve weeks later, he still seemed lost. With no clear job prospects, and tensions between himself and Libby at record highs, he looked ten years older than the previous time we had met.

Both Craig and Libby talked incessantly about their fears of the day when their savings account ran dry. "What if one of the boys breaks a leg once the insurance expires?" wondered Libby, who was underweight anyway and now looked positively emaciated. Her writing income would barely pay their mortgage costs, she said.

For all their troubles, though, when I asked them in separate interviews if they regretted ever having made the move in the first place, each answered no. And they gave the same reason: their experiences had forced them to expand their horizons in ways they otherwise never would.

Craig, in responding to my query, pulled out a list labeled "Transferable Skills," and another of occupations—real estate appraisal, mail order sales, office management—in which those skills could be put to good use. He explained that he had spent a good portion of his time since returning from Long Island preparing those lists. "Things were so tense at home, I'd go off to the library and work my way through the Richard Bolles book *What Color Is Your Parachute?*" Craig explained. "I would never have known about my potential for other fields if I hadn't been backed into this corner. Now I'm seriously considering leaving magazine publishing entirely, and the possibilities are really exciting."

More innovative still, Craig was also thinking about swapping roles with Libby—working part-time at one of the new professions from his list and taking over primary responsibility for the children and house while Libby served as chief breadwinner. For a couple of weeks Craig had been getting the children out of bed each morning, dressing and feeding them, and caring for them after they returned home from day camp as well.

Libby, during this same period, had met with the managing editor of the local newspaper about a possible thirty-hour-per-week job that would provide medical insurance benefits and still leave time for her free-lance writing.

"We're in an experimental stage now," Libby summed up. "We don't know what either of us is going to end up doing. When we left New York, we thought we could go directly from Point A to Point E. We found out you have to go through points

B, C, and D first, but I have this feeling the trip will have been worth it."

GETTING STUCK IN SECOND GEAR

The real casualties in career crashes are those people who do *not* move onward after their initial plans fail. Unlike Libby and Craig Mullen, they get stuck in second gear.

Among the most likely victims, ironically enough, are hard-nosed "macho men" who point with pride to their grit and independence. Lacking close friends and cut off from their emotions, they deal poorly with loss. Rather than confronting their tragedy head-on and seeking out alternatives, they spend their energies denying what happened and being angry.

I met several former middle managers who left their corporations rather than become members of what *Business Month* magazine dubbed "the new corporate underclass"—that growing stratum of talented managers whose odds of making it into an executive suite are about the same as winning the lottery. No matter how much talent they possess or how hard they work, they will never move very far up the corporate ladder. With so many positions eliminated from corporations over the last dozen years, and so many other overqualified people waiting in line for the few places that remain, many managers' careers permanently plateau before they reach age fifty.

Some middle managers reconcile themselves to life on the plateau. They accept the token raises and limited authority given them because they cannot imagine how they'd make a living if they left their companies. But other middle managers, possessed of entrepreneurial ambitions and chutzpah, tell their employers—in the words of the immortal country and western song—to take their job and shove it. Then off they go to start their own businesses.

Studies have found that entrepreneurship surges in cities where the largest companies have restructured. Some of the new businesses are started by people who have been laid off, but many are begun by managers who have survived the blood-letting and have chosen to break away from their ever meaner and leaner companies. The trend is evidenced in the astounding growth of *Entrepreneur* magazine between 1987 to 1990, a period in which advancement opportunities for middle managers plummeted. The circulation of *Entrepreneur* magazine rose 82 percent, to 325,000, during that three-year span.

The entrepreneurial alternative is not necessarily, however, the quick fix which magazines like *Entrepreneur* sometimes portray it to be. Fifty percent of small businesses do not survive beyond their first few years, and the number of small business failures has been rising. Dun & Bradstreet estimates that 97,000 businesses failed in 1992, up from 87,300 a year earlier, and 50,400 in 1989.

Behind every small business that collapses is an individual or a group of partners who banked their future on its success. The failure can leave them wasted, both financially and emotionally, for years.

Nick DeLucca, for instance, a man I interviewed in suburban Washington, D.C., will probably never fully erase the debt he incurred in starting his own housewares store. A year after shutting down his business, he has a drinking problem and little sense of self-direction. Interviewing Nick in the disheveled living room of his condominium, I felt myself to be in the presence of someone of great ability and drive whose will had been sapped.

A stocky, no-nonsense guy, Nick, thirty-six, still takes considerable pride in having quit his job as manager of a buying group at a large department store chain. "I was not being challenged or rewarded," he asserts, "and I wasn't going to stand for it. You get where you know more than the next guy, but the next guy's your boss. There were a lot of political moves taking place in management—people being directed on a faster track than I was, and I resented that."

Early on, when he first decided to leave the company, Nick considered changing employers rather than leaving corporate life entirely. Headhunters had approached him several times with opportunities to move to other parts of the country for jobs similar to the one he had.

A couple of events in his personal life motivated Nick to make the more extreme move of opening his own business. His father developed cancer, and over the course of the three months between the diagnosis and his death, Nick's perspective on his own life changed. The loss of his father prompted a desire in Nick to spend his remaining years more meaningfully. "I really felt I should do something to satisfy myself instead of working just to put in time and collect a paycheck," he explained.

During that same period, Nick split up with a woman he had been dating for a couple of years. "It all sort of clicked," he said. "I'd had a bug up my butt for years that I could put together a better-run business than the one I was working for. Now I didn't have the distraction of a demanding relationship, and having just lost my dad, I also thought I'd do something he'd have been proud of. He'd always encouraged me to take chances and stand up for myself."

When Nick asked friends and colleagues what they thought of his idea to open a housewares store, he was surprised and encouraged by their reactions. He had expected them to laugh in his face, but instead they responded in the flattering way people so often do to someone on the verge of becoming an independent entrepreneur. "They said they wished *they* had the nerve to go out on their own," Nick recollected. "Even one of the headhunters who had been trying to recruit me said to me, 'I'll be honest with you. If you want to open your own business, do it. You're at the right time in your life. You'll always regret it if you don't, and if it doesn't work out, you're still young enough to do something else.' "

TOUGH ODDS TO BEAT

Nick's business did fail—miserably. During the entire year his store was open, it never came within striking distance of showing a profit.

The failure took him completely off guard. Everyone he had consulted during the twelve months it took to set up the business—accountants, real estate brokers, bankers, marketing researchers, suppliers—thought he had a winner. The location he had selected in a new shopping mall being built next to a huge office complex in Alexandria, Virginia, seemed ideal for the up-market housewares store he was planning. White-collar customers would wander in during lunch and after work, he figured, and with fifteen years' experience as a buyer, Nick knew the merchandise that would appeal to them and how to price it.

Yet within a month of the grand opening, he could smell that something was wrong. An office glut hit northern Virginia, and the office building adjoining the mall sat one-third empty. As a result, the developer of the shopping mall had trouble finding tenants. Nick's shop sat like a lonely island; neither the storefront to one side of his nor the one directly across the mall was occupied.

Nick hung on, hoping first that the Christmas season would rescue him and that he could then pick up some of the local bridal market in the spring. "I went from being totally elated and proud of my accomplishment to becoming more worried and more determined than ever to beat the odds," he said in describing his emotional state during that period. "When we didn't break even for December, the worry started to outgun the determination. I started drinking more than I should, basically to get myself to sleep at night."

By the time the last day of June rolled around and Nick affixed his hand-lettered "Out of Business" sign to the front door of the store, he was on the verge of a serious alcohol problem. He was drinking close to a six-pack of beer every night.

Only lately—a year and a half since that day he closed the store—has Nick stopped boozing. With the help of an Alcoholics Anonymous chapter at a church down the road, he's gotten his drinking under control. His career, however, is another matter. He has been living off money remaining from his father's estate while searching in vain for a new line of work he can commit himself to.

In response to questions about his future plans, Nick rambled on about a wide range of careers he says he is seriously considering, from doing product development for a housewares manufacturer to going back to school and becoming a high school teacher. "Call it confidence in yourself, call it entrepreneurial drive—it's harder for me to feel that now," he acknowledged. "I'm somewhat bewildered about what exactly I will do. Sometimes it seems like I'm just going through the motions now. I send out résumés and talk to headhunters, but everything I turn up feels like a stopgap, not something I'd want for the long haul."

Like the person who leaves a bad marriage only to enter a rebound relationship that also collapses, Nick is left befuddled about what he really wants or is capable of. "Some days," he owned up, "I even wonder if I made a stupid mistake leaving the company in the first place. I felt stuck there, but no more stuck than I am right now."

Why can't Nick move forward? I suspect the answer lies in his refusal to face up to the tragedy of his business collapse.

Intellectually, he has accepted the fact that the shop went bust; he could hardly do otherwise, in light of the $150,000 he still owes his creditors. But emotionally, Nick has refused to come to terms with his career crash. He has adroitly managed to avoid nearly all the symptoms of a crash.

Nick's drinking masked the depression he otherwise would have felt during the months preceding and following the demise of the business. Like many traditionally masculine men, he found it easier to endure hangovers than feelings of failure and defeat.

As for the isolation people who are out of work usually encounter, when I arrived at Nick's condominium complex for our interview, it was like visiting a man in exile. The directions he had given me for locating his condo in the sprawling 200-unit complex got me utterly lost, and I couldn't find a soul to ask directions. Everybody was off at work.

Nick has taken steps to ensure he is virtually never alone or at home. He joined a gym, for one thing, where he works out each day with a group of guys about his age, several of whom are themselves unemployed, having quit, retired early, or been laid off. They serve as a kind of misery-loves-company support group for one another. Nick also volunteered to tutor students in arithmetic three afternoons a week at a school in Washington (ostensibly as part of his research into whether he'd like to become a teacher).

Nick did experience self-blame, the other emotional reaction that normally accompanies a career crash, after his business flopped. "I beat up on myself about errors I made, things I should have done differently," he admitted late in our discussion. "But I also realized that things happen you have no control over. The developer for the mall had misrepresented things, and the whole economy of the region was drifting downward.

"I equate it with cancer. You can be careful about what you eat and never smoke a cigarette a day in your life and still get cancer. Even with all my expertise and all the research I did, the business caught cancer and died."

Nick would like to believe that the only remaining costs from the death of his business are the loans he must repay, which he says are no big deal. "I just have to factor in nine hundred dollars a month for the next twenty years to pay back my business loans," he said. "Some people have education loans to pay off. I have these."

In truth, though, Nick is paying a far greater price—the price of denial. Carl Jung wrote in one of his essays: "There is no coming to consciousness without pain." By his refusal to feel the pain that normally accompanies a crash, Nick cannot get straight in his mind what went wrong in his recent past or what path he should take in the future.

QUITTERS SOMETIMES WIN

In careers, as in love, the odds of success immediately following a breakup are not great. Nick DeLucca and Craig Mullen are far from alone in having walked out of one bad situation into another. Most people, when they quit a career, make some poor choices before they find a good one.

Virtually everyone who leaves a career has war stories to tell about what happened subsequently. Fortunately, though, many stories have happy endings. Some people discover talents they never knew they had—talents they eventually put to good use in whole new occupations they never previously imagined they would enter.

Other people who leave their jobs to try something different end up returning to their previous line of work after their experiment fails, but in a new guise. A lawyer gave up a partnership in a corporate firm in order to go into advertising, which he ended up hating even more. Now he is happily practicing law again, but as a criminal defense attorney.

Then there are those whose tribulations after they quit their jobs gives them the strength and determination to pursue interests they abandoned long ago. One of the more inspiring such tales was relayed to me by Francine Sundlan, a forty-one-year-old laboratory technician at a pharmaceutical company in Minneapolis. At the time of our interview, Francine had just been accepted to medical school—a lifelong ambition she says she never would have fulfilled had she not quit her previous career and persevered through the tough times that followed.

"I never had the self-confidence until now. At the time I went to college in 1967, there weren't many options for women. My mother said, 'Why don't you be a teacher or a nurse?' So my sister became a teacher, and I became a nurse," Francine said, laughing at the inevitability of it all, but adding: "I did take the first year of premed, but then I wasn't sure I could cut it academically and I switched into the nursing program."

Francine worked as a nurse for eighteen years following her graduation from that program. As head nurse on a coronary care unit at a large hospital in Minneapolis, she was making good money when she resigned, but she felt so unchallenged, she knew what the doctors and other nurses were going to say before they said it. She had reached a state she refers to as "terminal boredom," and though she daydreamed of quitting, she didn't dare. She was divorced and had a teenage daughter to support.

It took a string of disturbing events at work and in her personal life, all occurring within a few weeks of one another, to dislodge her. First the health care conglomerate that owned the hospital where she worked brought in a new management team who initiated a series of cost-containment measures that saddled the nurses with more work. Then at home one night, Francine caught her daughter popping amphetamines in the bathroom. And finally, "The thing that actually mobilized me, I was driving home one night in December and it was windy and snowing very hard—I mean it was like someone had thrown a sheet over your windshield—and a car skidded into my rear and almost sent me through the windshield. I got out of the car and I said, 'That's it. I've got to take my future into my own hands and get out of Minnesota before it kills me and my daughter both.' "

The next day Francine called an old friend who had moved to Atlanta and asked her if she could find her a job down there. "I told her I'd do most anything other than nursing," Francine remembers.

Francine prepared a résumé emphasizing her administrative experience, copies of which her friend, a former nurse herself, mailed off to advertisers in the Help Wanted sections of Atlanta newspapers. A week later Francine's telephone rang during dinner, and a man identifying himself as a doctor in a university research center in Atlanta asked if she would be interested in managing the staff at a hematology research laboratory.

She flew to Atlanta to be interviewed, was hired on the spot, and three weeks later, Francine, who had lived in Minneapolis all her life, moved herself and her fifteen-year-old daughter halfway across the country.

Francine felt she had a new lease on life. Not only had she gotten out of nursing for an interesting job at a higher salary, she had left Minneapolis. "On the verge of my fortieth birthday, I finally grew up and left my hometown," she related.

So buoyed was Francine that she ignored clear warning signs of trouble at work. Her first week on the job, her boss made comments to her about another woman in the lab dressing provocatively, and Francine wrote it off as his awkward way of making conversation. "But then," she recalls with disgust, "he started coming in and saying things to me like, 'I dreamt I had sex with you last night.' I just thought, 'That's so inappropriate,' but I wouldn't do anything about it."

Francine had never experienced sexual harassment on the job. Now that she was being hassled, she didn't know what to do except ignore it and hope it would stop.

Instead, the harassment escalated. Her boss started asking her out to dinner, and when she declined, he took revenge by undermining her authority with the staff she supervised.

Frightened and unsure of what to do, Francine became immobilized. In her job at the lab, she had trouble deciding which supplies to buy or whom to hire, and at home, "I could hardly decide what to make for dinner," she recollects. "I blamed myself for not investigating the job better. Why didn't I ask more about my prospective employer? I felt what was happening to me was proof that I'd had no right to make a big move like that."

Ironically, Francine was suffering the all-out career crash that for years she had staved off. She was depressed, she was blaming herself for her troubles—and it's hard to imagine how she could have felt more isolated. In a city where she knew virtually no one, and in a job where she had no friends, Francine didn't know where to turn. She considered registering a complaint with someone higher up in the medical school administration but thought better of the idea. "It would have been my word against his. There was never an audience when he said things to me. And I was so depressed by then, and so down on myself, I didn't feel like I could handle it if I was challenged."

Only two months after setting foot in Georgia, before she'd unpacked the last box, Francine decided to return to Minneapolis. When her boss started calling her at home and she had to fend him off in front of her daughter, she knew she had little other choice.

But Francine did not pick up her old life exactly where she had left off. She turned down an offer to return to her old nursing job and took instead the job as laboratory technician she still holds. It pays less well, she says, but in other regards has turned out to be a gold mine. Her supervisor gave her responsibilities above what her title would indicate, which helped rebuild Francine's ego. And one of Francine's co-workers, upon hearing her saga of what happened in Atlanta, offered to call a lawyer she knew who specializes in harassment suits.

Francine says that once she met with that attorney and "resolved to take on Goliath," her life turned around. "Once I started fighting back, I no longer felt so shamed and defeated by what had happened, and my relationship with my daughter also improved.

"She was in the other room one night while I was meeting with the lawyer," Francine recounted, "and she came out afterward and she said, 'I really learned a lot, Mom. You don't have to just always accept it if people treat you badly. You can take action.'"

Francine had to withdraw money from her retirement fund to pay the lawyer's $6,000 retainer fee. And although at the time I interviewed her, about fourteen months after she hired the lawyer, no court date had been set, Francine already felt victorious. "Even if we don't get the settlement we're after, I'll always know I made that bastard pay a price for what he did. He might think twice before harassing other women who work for him."

Twice brave and feeling like a winner, Francine now had little difficulty taking a long overdue step to make good on her girlhood dream of becoming a doctor. She enrolled in a refresher course to prepare for the Medical College Admissions Test, scored high, and located a couple of medical schools that offer special fellowships for returning women. On the day of our interview, she was packing her belongings to move to one of those schools, where she would begin her studies in a few weeks.

Francine's daughter, too, was packing to go off to school. She had turned her grades around during her last two years of high school and gained admission to the University of Minnesota, where she will live in the dorms.

"She plans to major in premed," Francine said triumphantly.

WHEN COUPLES
CRASH

Many times when baby boomers lose or leave their jobs, more is going on than meets the eye. At first glance they seem simply to have been fired or grown tired of their work. But on closer inspection a more complex picture emerges.

Among the married people I interviewed, for instance, career crashes were often synchronized. First one partner would quit a job or get fired, and then, within a few years, the other would follow suit.*

Perhaps people prone to career crashes marry others of the same bent. Or maybe what psychologists call the "contagion effect" operates in these households. Humans, like other animals, emulate the behaviors of those around them.

In some marriages, however, something additional operates to provoke sequential crashes—something unique to dual-career baby boomer relationships. Marriages between baby

---

*I use the word "married" as a convenient shorthand. The patterns discussed in this chapter also occur within long-term relationships where the partners are not legally married.

boomer professionals are typically founded on an ideology of equality and reciprocity. In principle, if not always in practice, the partners evenly share all burdens and perquisites that befall them. So if one partner radically alters his or her career course, the other has an implicit right to do the same.

Much as baby boomer partners believe in alternating who changes the baby's diapers, cooks the evening meal, or drives the older car, so too do they see virtue in trading off the duty to be responsibly employed. If I got out of bed at three o'clock last night to comfort the baby, my partner is obliged to do so tonight; if last year my partner left a job she hated to start her own business, this year she should permit me to do the same.

A kind of waltz of entitlements takes place within baby boomer marriages. Repeatedly, when I interviewed married couples, in the midst of explaining why they crashed out of their careers when they did, they would say: "It was my turn." Some said they had been the main breadwinner in the family long enough. Others said it was their turn to make a change because they had helped their partner through a career transition at some point in the past.

DARCY AND MIKE: WHO'S TO PAY?

Within the past couple of years, Darcy Bishop, thirty-four, and her husband, Mike Witter, thirty-five, have each resigned from a good job, she at a leading newspaper, he at a prominent Seattle architecture firm.

Mike was the first to quit, and early in our conversation he attributed his decision to career concerns. "I'd started with the firm right out of college, and they still thought of me as a beginning draftsman, even though I'd been there ten years and directed several projects. I couldn't express myself there.

Somebody was always looking over my shoulder, telling me what to do, and they were bringing in new people over me who weren't as good as I was," Mike said.

But later in our interview, which took place in Mike's home office, he revealed another reason he resigned and started his own firm. "When we lost the baby, that was really tough," Mike said somberly, referring to Darcy's miscarriage two years earlier. "It was hard on Darcy, obviously, but I think the whole experience was even more devastating for me than for her. I realized we were going to have only one child, and it became superimportant to me to spend time with our son, Matthew, who had just turned three."

So Mike announced to Darcy he wanted to turn the garage into an office and go out on his own. Because he would probably make little if any money the first year or two, he told her, she would have to earn more money than she had been if the family was to maintain its current lifestyle.

Mike and Darcy both knew that she had the ability to make more money. For several years prior to meeting Mike, she had lived in New York and worked as an editor at a national women's magazine. But then, during a visit home to Seattle one Thanksgiving to see her parents, she met Mike and fell in love. Following a brief long-distance courtship, Darcy decided to move back to the town where she'd grown up, and she took an $18,000-a-year job editing a small regional magazine.

It was a job Darcy enjoyed in spite of the pay, partly because it reintegrated her into the community, and partly because it was refreshingly low-pressured compared to her job in New York. All the same, Darcy willingly agreed to Mike's request that she seek a better-paid position. She was moved, she told me in a separate interview, by her husband's desire to be with their son, and by the fact that he had been the major moneymaker thus far in their marriage. Besides, after the miscarriage she was feeling somewhat inadequate, she also let me know, and she welcomed a new career challenge.

Darcy found the job at the newspaper after less than a month of networking, and both she and Mike described the year that followed as a glorious time in their professional and personal lives. Although the work was demanding and seldom confined to a forty-hour week, Darcy felt she was learning a lot in her job as editor of a weekly section of the newspaper. And Mike, though he landed only a handful of small jobs during that period, loved working for himself.

As a couple, the two of them grew closer than they had ever been. Each night they compared notes from their jobs over dinner, and every Sunday they set aside as "family day" to go hiking or boating with Matthew.

When Darcy learned she was pregnant, almost precisely on the first anniversary of the day she began her new job, they were both thrilled: the missing piece of their dream—a second child—might yet become reality. For the first trimester of her pregnancy, they tried to curb their optimism, remembering how traumatic the earlier miscarriage had been. Once Darcy carried the pregnancy without a hitch into the fourth and then the fifth months, though, they started talking about names for the child and how they might decorate her room.

Then at the start of Darcy's final trimester she woke up one morning bleeding. She rushed to the obstetrician, who hospitalized her for a week, at the end of which the fetus died.

Mike and Darcy were crushed. At first, their grief brought them closer together, but after some time the emotional strains took a toll. They had trouble sleeping at night, their work suffered, and before long they were quarreling with each other every evening. One rainy night Darcy threw the clothes Mike had left on the bedroom floor out the window. Another night Mike threw the telephone against the wall after Darcy criticized him for not being more aggressive with a potential client.

Then Matthew, responding to the tensions between his parents in the way five-year-olds sometimes do, contracted a series of respiratory illnesses that culminated in a brief hospitalization for pneumonia.

A CRASH OF HER OWN

Immediately upon Matthew's return home, Darcy claimed rights to a career crash of her own. She notified her husband she was going to quit her job to write a novel.

"I told Mike, 'I've had it,'" Darcy quoted herself as having said six weeks prior to our interview. "'I've lost two pregnancies, I've been working sixty hours a week, and I'm exhausted. I'm throwing the ball back in your court. *You* pay the bills. I'm staying home with my kid.'"

Darcy, who gave her boss at the newspaper only two weeks' notice of her departure, said she had been disillusioned with her job for a couple of months. In addition to having to work longer hours than she had been promised when she was hired, she'd come to feel she wasn't being given enough autonomy over the section she edited. She also found herself jealous of Mike for his close bond with Matthew.

But Darcy's decision to quit her job and work from home was not as favorably received as Mike's similar decision had been two years earlier.

Not only Mike but also Darcy's mother let her know they considered the move precipitous and out of character. If she felt so stressed out by the miscarriage and the job, at least she could have waited a little while, they suggested. At the time she quit, Mike had only a couple of small jobs under contract; they still needed her income. Besides, Darcy had always worked, her husband and mother pointed out; why this sudden urge to stay home and be supported by her husband?

In her interview with me, which was conducted in the kitchen while Mike played with Matthew in the backyard, Darcy conceded that, indeed, her timing had not been optimal. "I quit right after Mike lost a big job he'd been counting on, and things got pretty hairy," she said. They missed a mortgage payment, she relayed, and at one point a few weeks ago they had to clean out change from the bottom of the dresser drawers to buy groceries.

"It has been a stressful time, but it has lit a fire under Mike, which he needed," Darcy went on. "He'd been dragging his feet getting the firm moving. He'd spend half his workday with Matthew, and when I'd hear him on the phone at night with potential clients, he just wasn't pushing hard enough."

Darcy said Mike finally got motivated when it looked like they were either going to have to go hungry or borrow money from her folks. Two weeks before our meeting, he signed up a big job that would support them for the coming six or eight months.

WOMEN OPTING OUT

If Darcy accepts her mother's and husband's criticism that her timing was bad, she flatly rejects the notion that she has regressed to some sort of prefeminist state by deciding to return home to write her novel. "This was a very assertive thing for me to do," she said. "I've never been without a job since I was sixteen years old, so I think it's pretty gutsy of me just to up and leave like that."

Darcy characterized her decision to return home as an effort to better integrate her professional and maternal sides. "I've burned out on being an editor and need some time to feel like a mom and to see if I have any talent as a fiction writer," she said.

One of the great surprises for me during the course of my re-search was meeting about a dozen women like Darcy, women who had left full-time careers, were mostly or totally living on a man's income, and took considerable pride in depending on their husbands.

As recently as the mid-1980s, when Arlie Hochschild conducted interviews with working mothers for her book *The Second Shift*, few career women would voluntarily trade in their briefcases for an apron. Many of the women Hochschild surveyed indicated they would be bored or "go bananas" if they stayed home all day.

"Paid work has come to seem exciting, life at home dull," Hochschild reported in her 1989 book.

Throughout the 1980s, a woman with a college education and good job prospects whose principal occupation was that of homemaker could expect to be viewed like a leper. In a 1985 survey of the alumni of Harvard and Stanford, nearly half of the people questioned said that women who stayed at home were less respected than women who worked. "If you want to know what shunning feels like, go to a cocktail party, and when they ask you what you do, say 'I'm a housewife,' " said a woman in Hochschild's study who had just quit her job.

By the 1990s, however, women in certain circles who decided to stay home were no longer so much shunned as they were used as sounding boards. "My three close friends are women in the position I was in before I left the firm," Tracy Collins, a thirty-four-year-old graduate of Harvard Law School who does legal writing part-time and takes care of her young daughter, told me. "When we get together, I hear them say the same thing I used to say: 'When I'm at the office, I wish I were at home.' They don't really enjoy the law, and they have husbands who make good money, but they're afraid to quit."

In upper-income, two-earner families, 68 percent of the second paycheck goes to child care, household help, clothing, transportation, and other work-related costs, a 1992 study found. Yet for every woman unhappy in a job who has taken advantage of the opportunity her husband's income affords her to leave, probably fifty or a hundred others have not even allowed themselves to contemplate such a possibility. Their situation is strangely reminiscent of a group of American women from the not so distant past, whom Betty Friedan described as suffering "a strange stirring, a sense of dissatisfaction, a yearning."

"Each suburban wife struggled with it alone," Friedan wrote in 1963 in *The Feminine Mystique*. "As she made the beds, shopped for groceries, matched slipcover material, ate peanut butter sandwiches with her children, chauffeured Cub Scouts and Brownies, lay beside her husband at night—she was afraid to ask even of herself the silent question—'Is this all?'"

Now, three decades later, some of the daughters of Friedan's wives are feeling their own stirrings. As they write memos, sit in meetings, count up frequent-flyer miles, and come home at seven o'clock or later, they ask their own version of the question "Is this all?" If they dislike their work or their bosses, if they resent the interminable hours, if they tire of postponing pregnancy or have children they seldom see, inevitably they lose faith that their careers will fulfill them.

At the same time, like Friedan's housewives a generation earlier, they may hesitate to acknowledge those feelings. If they stay home, will they turn into the depressed housewives their mothers had warned them not to become?

But it is not simply their own fears they must contend with; they must also confront a chorus of other voices warning them not to leave their careers behind. "Our fathers and mothers (who underwrote our higher education) remind us that our 'careers won't wait forever' and we 'didn't go to college for nothing,'" Kim Triedman, a twenty-nine-year-old video producer, wrote in a *Ms* magazine article about her decision to stay home with her daughter. "Our employers give us explicit policy on maternity leave—and subtler shows of our bosses' displeasure. Our husbands let us know that the mortgage is due and our bank balances are dropping."

THE NEW DOUBLE STANDARD

My interviews suggest that husbands, in particular, can present an obstacle. On the one hand, I met women who cite their husbands' opposition as the primary reason they remain in cheerless jobs instead of going part-time or taking a total break from work. I also met several women who *did* junk their jobs only to find that the toughest part was dealing with their husbands' reactions.

To understand why, we need only return to the Darcy Bishop–Mike Witter household in Seattle. Mike, generally a mild-mannered guy, has been hopping mad the last couple of months since Darcy returned home. "If I'd wanted a housewife I wouldn't have married a career woman," he said. "If Darcy wanted a macho provider type, she shouldn't have married me."

Having been married for three years in his early twenties to a woman he described as possessing "no larger ambition in life than to stay home and have babies," Mike spent the five years between his divorce and the time he met Darcy searching for a totally different sort of mate. Darcy, who'd made it on her own in a tough industry in New York City, filled the bill perfectly. The last thing he ever expected her to do was become a hausfrau.

While some men are content to support their wives in exchange for a partial exemption from housework or to avoid competing with them professionally, others, like Mike Witter, are not. When their wives leave jobs, these men feel cheated and betrayed as surely as they would if a spouse were having an affair. From the husbands' point of view, a promise has been broken.

From the wives' perspective, on the other hand, no such promise ever existed. As one of my interviewees remarked, "I don't recall taking a wedding vow to love, honor, and financially support him."

What we have here might be called the new double standard, but this time it is one the sexes share. A man objects to his wife returning home even though he grants himself that privilege; a woman asserts her right to put parenthood above career even as she denies her husband that opportunity.

A DELICATE BALANCE

Lisa Silberstein, Ph.D., a Yale University psychologist, pinpointed what may be the fundamental contradiction in dual-career baby boomer marriages. In an intensive study of twenty couples aged thirty-two to forty-two, all of whom have children, Silberstein discovered that neither the men nor the women had forsaken their old-fashioned notions about husbands' and wives' roles; they'd merely added newfangled expectations on top. The women took for granted that their husbands would be the chief breadwinners and make more money, even as they called upon them to share equally in child rearing and housekeeping. And the men still assumed their wives would take primary responsibility for homemaking, even as they counted upon them to contribute substantially to the family income.

Baby boomers expect to have a traditional and a modern marriage at the same time, Silberstein suggests.

Her study included some couples who actually managed to accommodate these conflicting expectations and live happily together for long periods of time. The husbands provided what

Silberstein calls "the solid, base income" and also did a great deal around the house; and the wives served as chief nurturers and family managers and at the same time maintained substantial careers.

But the applecart is easily upset, Silberstein told me. "Complications come when things become lopsided, when one career is progressing at a clip and the other is either faltering or falling off," she said.

The system depends upon husbands doing very well at work and wives maintaining their careers. If the man slips at all, or if the woman slips very far—or conversely, if she does *too* well—tensions quickly mount. "Women say it is hard for them to enjoy their own careers if their husband's is going poorly," Silberstein reported, "and men say they have doubts about whether the marriage will survive when they are doing less well than their wives."

Both the wives and the husbands were less alarmed by declines in the woman's career than in the man's, Silberstein indicated, especially if these declines followed the birth of a child. But wives' careers were not viewed as *dispensable* by either party. Men told Silberstein that their wives' income gave them leeway to take risks in their own careers, and women spoke of the centrality of their professional accomplishments to their self-esteem.

As sociologist Rosanna Hertz, the author of *More Equal than Others: Women and Men in Dual-Career Marriages,* has observed, "In most cases, the development of careers is alternating in character. His career comes first and makes possible hers or investments leading to hers. Her career makes possible shifts in his career. Perhaps more important than the alternation of investments is the fact that the large and stable portion of family income coming from the wife's career makes possible career shifts for him. Because the dual-career marriage frees men from sole economic responsibility, the men can be less obsessed by work, less aggressive, and even less motivated because the weight of this responsibility is shared."

Thus two partners stand to benefit substantially from each other's careers, so long as both careers are going reasonably well. When they are, dual-career spouses tend to be very supportive and appreciative of each other. If either career takes a dive, however, all that good will may quickly evaporate. "The cheering is predicated on feeling good about oneself," Silberstein notes. "When one person's career isn't going well, he or she is going to have a lot of trouble cheering the person whose career *is* going well."

When either a wife's or a husband's career stumbles, some unwelcome emotions bubble to the surface. "Comparisons and competition become intense and make the partners very uncomfortable," said Silberstein, pointing out that ordinarily, baby boomer partners manage to avoid experiencing themselves in competition with each other. The men and women she studied made a point of telling her they had gone into different fields, different companies, or separate divisions within the same company to bypass competition with each other.

"For women, the idea of competing with anyone, let alone their husbands, is fairly distasteful," Silberstein said. "And for men, although competition may be something they are socialized to do, it's not with women that men are encouraged to compete, but with men—and they're certainly not socialized to compete with their own wives."

SERIAL BREADWINNING

Perhaps it's no accident that the couple in my research who most adeptly resolved their career-related conflicts was gay. Less encumbered than a straight couple by the burdens of traditional versus modern and male versus female roles, these men came up with a creative way to resolve the dilemmas posed by their careers falling out of sync.

They actually made an agreement to trade off responsibility for being primary breadwinner every couple of years. "He's the Sugar Daddy right now. Then in another year, it's my obligation to be Sugar Daddy again," said Rick Ruiz, a tenured professor who several years ago grew so tired of teaching he took an indefinite sabbatical from the university. For over a year he did little but hike and read, until his partner got fed up and threatened to stop paying the bills.

After a long period of haggling, the two of them devised their work-cycling scheme. Although Rick's partner, a physician, is devoted to his work and does not share the urge to retire, he has eagerly accepted the arrangement. During the year when he is relieved of the obligation to make money, he plans to take a leave from his private practice to volunteer part-time in an AIDS clinic while devoting the rest of his time to what he dubs his "tennis addiction."

These two people are obviously in a rare and enviable position: their places of employment allow them to take periodic leaves, and having no children, they can live on one income. But other couples without those advantages (including straight couples) also survived potentially lethal career crashes to move forward in their relationships.

THE THOMPSONS PRIOR TO COUNSELING

One of these couples was Barbara and Doug Thompson of Sacramento, California. The Thompsons had been together fifteen years and gone through several horribly tense periods before they went to a marriage counselor for help. Over margaritas at a Mexican restaurant a year after the last of their sessions with the counselor, each of them told me what they had learned about their fundamental clash in career orientations—the trouble it generated between them over the years until they finally resolved it.

"With twenty-twenty hindsight, I realize the problem was obvious from the first moment we met," said Barbara, thirty-eight, a short, spirited, curly-haired brunette I interviewed while her husband was off shopping with their seven-year-old son and infant daughter. "Doug was driving a bus for the senior citizens center where I was an assistant administrator."

The year was 1975, and Barbara had graduated Phi Beta Kappa from Northwestern University a few months earlier. At the time she met Doug, she was dating a man she describes as boring and egotistical, but possessed of two key qualities her parents had urged her to look for in a boyfriend—he was Jewish and he was in medical school. Doug, on the other hand, came from a blue-collar Protestant family and had dropped out of the University of Illinois a few years earlier. "No question about it," said Barbara with a mischievous grin, "dating him was a little act of rebellion on my part at first. He was different from anybody I'd ever dated, and he was a great lover.

"He was also a challenge," she added. "As soon as you talked with the guy for five minutes you saw he was bright. I never expected to make a bank president or a brain surgeon out of him, but I did think I could bring some direction to his life."

After a few months of dating, when Doug proposed they live together, Barbara gave him an ultimatum. "We were walking on the beach by Lake Michigan," she recalled, "and I said to him, 'I really love you, but you're not motivated to do anything, and I need someone who's going to make something of himself. It's never going to work if all you're ever going to be is a bus driver.' "

Highly ambitious herself and striding rapidly toward her goal of becoming director of a hospital, Barbara helped Doug find a program where he could finish his bachelor's degree at night in a couple of semesters. Then she encouraged him to go on to graduate school and offered to relocate to wherever he was admitted.

Doug opted for a master's degree program in educational psychology at the University of California at Davis, a place that turned out to be disastrous for Barbara. Nowhere within driving distance could she find a job in her field.

"We lived in the graduate-student ghetto next to campus. Doug went off to school all day every day, and I was just miserable," Barbara related. Finally, in their fifth month there, the personnel director at a Sacramento hospital where she had applied for an administrative post offered her a job in the public relations department at half what she'd been making in Chicago, and she accepted. "I imagined P.R. involved taking people for lunches, being nice and smiling, and I figured I could do all that," Barbara remembers thinking the day when she switched into the profession where she has remained ever since.

But that first public relations job was dreadfully dull. Mostly Barbara wrote notices about employees who had been hired or retired and took schoolchildren on tours of the facility.

"It seems like Doug and I are always in a state where one or the other of us is not really happy in our work," said Barbara, in a refrain I heard often in my conversations with couples in which both partners had suffered career crashes.

Unhappiness over careers is seldom divided equally, however, within a relationship. Over time, one partner tends to emerge as the career malingerer more so than the other. And within the Thompsons' marriage, that person was Doug. From the start Barbara was the career-oriented partner, Doug the anguished wanderer. Those first months in Davis were but a temporary aberration.

Less than a year into his graduate studies, Doug began making noises about not wanting to complete his degree, and Barbara began treating her job as a launching pad for something better. She invited reporters from local newspapers and radio and television stations out to lunch; she joined an organization for women communications professionals; she volunteered her talents to the local Planned Parenthood organization.

By the end of their first year in Davis, Barbara had gotten a good job in public relations at a television station and Doug had dropped out of school.

MR. MOM

Doug, who is forty-two, has trouble explaining why, upon leaving the graduate program, he chose to take a job in the personnel department at a large manufacturing company. "It was the only job I could find that paid halfway decent, where I could work directly with people," he offered during my separate conversation with him at the same restaurant after Barbara and I had finished talking and she had left with the children.

But whatever had led Doug into that personnel job back in 1979, he never much liked it, and he fought a lot with his boss. "He was basically inept as a manager, and tact not being my forte, I told him so," said Doug.

He has learned to be more diplomatic in the past couple of years, Doug went on to explain, following the loss of that and two subsequent jobs. After the manufacturing company, Doug went to work in the human resources department of a large insurance firm. Prior to taking that position, he made a vow to Barbara to mind his mouth, and for a couple of years he kept his word—until a new vice president came on board whom Doug considered autocratic. In what Doug thought was a clever political move, he started feeding stories about this VP's inappropriate conduct to a more senior vice president in the company. The end result was that neither man trusted Doug, and in a round of staff cuts, they eliminated his job.

"I don't know which feeling was strongest—shock, depression, or anger," Doug said of the morning his pink slip arrived. In the period that followed, he found himself unmotivated to find another job and performed poorly when he went on interviews.

Then, after three months of searching for jobs he knew he neither wanted nor would be offered, he determined to stay home for a while instead and be a full-time parent to their son, Josh, who had been conceived soon after Doug got the insurance company job and who was then about eighteen months old. "My pride had taken a bad beating, and I didn't want to go into anything remotely close to what I had just experienced, so it seemed like the wisest thing to do," Doug explained.

He remembers experiencing a real sense of contentment the first several weeks after he abandoned his job search and took Josh out of day care. At that time in the mid-1980s, the media was full of stories about the New Man who stays home with the kids and develops his feminine side. Doug felt like something of a courageous pioneer.

The only problem was, his wife had a very different view of the matter. "Barbara had been understanding and supportive and all that other good stuff after I lost my job, but once I stopped seeking other employment, she was on me all the time. 'We have a child and a mortgage,'" he said in a mock falsetto voice. "'If you think I'm going to support this family by myself, you can forget it.'"

Yet in spite of Barbara's reproaches, for close to half a year Doug refused to budge and go look for a job. During their heated arguments over that time, he held his moral ground, accusing her of "malicious yuppieism" for spending too little time with their son. As far as Doug was concerned, he contributed plenty to the family. From 7:30 A.M. until at least 6 P.M. every weekday he took care of Josh while Barbara, by then the director of public relations at the television station, worked. And on weekends, when he wasn't playing golf (a passion he'd acquired during his days at the insurance company job), he built a den in the basement.

Eventually, though, under pressure not only from his wife but from several male friends as well, Doug sought and landed another job.

It was when he lost that position—during his sixth month as an employment specialist with a state agency—that Barbara insisted he go with her to a marriage counselor.

THE THOMPSONS IN COUNSELING

To help the Thompsons stop fighting, the marriage counselor used one of the most valuable tools of his trade. He traced their attitudes toward work back to their relationships with their parents. By reframing their conflict outside the context of their marriage, he defused the tensions between them.

Barbara and Doug actually came to respect each other's positions. "Before we went for counseling, I thought Doug had developed his knack for butting heads with bosses just to torture me," said Barbara during our interview, "but it wasn't like that at all. He was being loyal to his father. His dad had been a factory worker who bragged to his sons about never taking any lip from anybody."

She herself was carrying on a family tradition, too, Barbara said. "I'm very ambitious, I'm my parents' only child—my father's a hotshot attorney and my mother's one of the top psychoanalysts on Long Island."

When Doug described what he learned during the marriage-counseling sessions, he, too, pointed up differences between their two families. "You know that old saying, 'Some people work to live, other people live to work'? Well, that about sums it up," said Doug. "Barb's mom and dad live to work, they get a real high off their work, and Barb's the same way. Whereas my dad worked in a Ford plant—lost a finger there one time. He lived for the end of the day when he could go off and get sloshed with his buddies."

Doug suggested that his father's drunkenness had had a big impact on him. While recognizing the point Barbara made about being loyal to his father's blue-collar pride, Doug also took from the marriage-counseling sessions an appreciation for the flip side of that coin—the ways in which his behavior toward bosses represent a *rejection* of his dad. "When he got drunk, he was a scary son of a bitch," Doug relayed. "If he said 'jump,' you asked, 'How high?' There was no room for questioning and debate. You'd do it right away, and you'd do it his way, or you'd find yourself on the other side of the room."

As an adult, whenever he was confronted by an authoritarian or excitable boss, Doug's spontaneous, self-protective response was to strike out. To refrain from doing so would have meant being thrust back into the horribly vulnerable position he knew as a child—the terrified little boy at the mercy of the big and capricious father.

Doug said he believes his zeal to be a good and involved parent, as well as his anger with Barbara for giving short shrift to parenting, are reactions to his relationship with his father.

MEETING EACH OTHER HALFWAY

Once the Thompsons stopped viewing each other's career inclinations judgmentally, they were open to the marriage counselor's suggestion that they explore what each of them *really* wanted from their work lives. With the counselor's help, they pinpointed what they were after for themselves and from each other.

Doug determined that although he would probably never become very ambitious, for the sake of his family and his own self-respect, he needed a job that provided a respectable income. He also decided to look for a position where he could be his own boss and have flexible hours. After considering a variety of options, from buying a fast food franchise to independent personnel consulting, he ended up in a line of work the very thought of which would have made him gag when he was younger. He sells insurance. "My idea of an insurance man was the snake-oil salesman, but it doesn't have to be that way," he said. "I only sell good products, so I get the personal satisfaction of helping people. And if I want to go off at three in the afternoon to coach my son's soccer team or play a round of golf, I can."

Meanwhile, Barbara's self-probing resulted in an even bigger surprise. She decided to have another child and ease up on her career for a few years. For the past year she's been working part-time, from 9 A.M. to 2 P.M., in a small public relations firm. Most of the rest of her time she spends with her son, who recently entered second grade, and her daughter, who is now fourteen months old.

"I'd been wanting this, secretly, since the morning I dropped my older son off for the first day of kindergarten. I'd cried all the way to the office. I felt like I was missing his childhood," she said. "But it took the seal of approval from a certified marriage counselor before I could give myself permission to slow down my career."

In essence, what the Thompsons have done is to meet each other halfway on both the career and domestic fronts. Workwise, Barbara has shifted her professional drive from first to second gear while Doug has gone from neutral to third. In their relationship, they have both moved from annoyance over their differences to an appreciation of what those differences contribute to the marriage.

Said Barbara: "I used to come home after a long day at the TV station and he'd be watching TV with a beer in his hand and Josh on his knee, and I'd think to myself, 'I married a bum. He should be out schmoozing and making connections.' Now I see him and I think, 'He's there for my kids.' I see so many marriages where the husband isn't even there, and Doug's there at night; he's an incredibly good father."

Said Doug: "When you're in a self-employed sales job, it's real helpful to have a wife who'll kick your butt if you get lazy. Barbara has more of a natural entrepreneurial spirit than I do, and just living with her, some of it rubs off on me."

Best of all, in spite of the adjustments they've made, the Thompsons have not sacrificed their individual dreams. "I still intend to be the top-ranked PR person in this town, but by age forty-five instead of forty," said Barbara.

"If I had my way, I'd be totally retired now and spend all my hours with my kids or on the golf course, but I'm going to have to wait until I'm fifty-five and the kids are out of college," Doug said, taking a small slip of paper out of his breast pocket.

"Of course if I win the lottery, it will be considerably sooner," he added with a slightly devilish smile.

part two

Delayed

Reactions

CHAPTER 5

PREMATURE
FORECLOSURE

If complications at home or at work cause many career crashes, the genesis of others lies in the distant past.

Picture this. At the tender age of eight or ten or twelve, you decide which profession you'll go into. In high school you study hard, and in college you take the right classes and participate in the right extracurricular activities to guarantee admission to a top-flight professional school.

A few years later you graduate near the top of your class and get a good job in law, business, or engineering. For the remainder of your twenties you devote yourself to making it in your profession.

Now you're in your thirties and reaping the rewards of your labors. At a time when many people your age are either out of work entirely or struggling to retain unrewarding jobs, you're well paid, well liked by your colleagues and superiors, and in line for more promotions.

Why then, seemingly out of the blue, do you start to dread going in to the office and spend the better part of every day anxious or depressed? Why, at home at night, do you have trouble sleeping?

Try to answer those questions and you draw a blank. Regardless of where you turn, there's no obvious reason for your unhappiness. Nothing has come up in your personal life to upset you—no sudden illness of a loved one, no new problems in your relationship. At work some minor annoyances may have arisen—assignments you don't enjoy, co-workers who get on your nerves. But these aren't serious enough to have thrown you so completely off balance.

A HOME AT WORK

This real-life nightmare proves difficult for most people to decode on their own, according to career counselors and therapists. Because the root of the problem lies in childhood, current misfortunes at home or at work largely are beside the point.

"Some people—I call them *prematurely foreclosed*—choose their careers too early, without first exploring who they are. They decide when they are eleven years old that they're going to be engineers or accountants," Judith Grutter, a career adviser in Pasadena and a past president of the California Career Development Association, told me. "Everything goes fine until their thirties, when they begin to discover that what they're doing doesn't make them entirely happy."

Usually the reason young people prematurely foreclose their options is to escape frightening situations at home that range all the way from parental violence to a mother or father who is chronically depressed. By entering a career track a child exits— symbolically at least—his or her family. Notes Amy Bloom, MSW, a therapist in Middletown, Connecticut: "In the same way that young women once got married, hoping their husbands would protect them, there are people who went toward their career hoping it would protect them from their families and keep them from becoming whoever they might become if they didn't have this structure to hold on to.

"But when they get older," adds Bloom, "they discover that their career is just a defense, and like most defenses, it leaks." When it does, their suppressed pain from childhood seeps out.

The most dramatic examples are found among children of abusive or alcoholic parents. A common way for such children to extricate themselves is to redirect their energies outside the family. Some get strung out on drugs and spend their time with other delinquent kids, others get pregnant. But another group breaks away by means of their intellect. They focus exclusively on their schoolwork when they are growing up, and once they leave home, on their careers.

Evelyn Breen of Boston is a case in point. To those she worked with, her collapse at age thirty-two came as a complete surprise. How could someone with such a promising future, who seemed so sound and rational, try to commit suicide and end up in a psychiatric hospital? With a degree from MIT and exceptional talents in electrical engineering, Evelyn was among the leading engineers of her generation.

True, she tended to keep to herself, but everyone assumed that was because she was wrapped up in her work. She never seemed depressed or missed work; in fact, she used to make jokes about how many "all nighters" she pulled to keep her projects on schedule.

But during our interview a year after her crash, when she was starting to put her life back together, Evelyn confided she had had her own private reasons for isolating herself and working those eighty-hour weeks. As a child she had learned that the only place she felt safe and secure was alone doing her work. Only there could she be fairly confident that her mother—who was authoritarian and abusive—wouldn't harm her. Were Evelyn to go out and play with her sister or with kids in the neighborhood, she might do something that would incur her mother's wrath. More often than not, her mother would accuse her of being too noisy and punish her, sometimes beating her with a belt. One time Evelyn's mother hit her so hard that she knocked her unconscious.

By the time Evelyn was in grade school, she had developed a modus operandi that protected her from her mother and even won her mother's praise. She barricaded herself in her room to study and rarely played with other kids.

Evelyn's posture of keeping strictly to her studies earned her high scores, scholarships, and honors clear through graduate school and into her career. Her work was so consuming that she scarcely noticed the missing pieces in her life.

But a pair of events sent Evelyn over the edge. First there was the visit to her parents in Phoenix at Christmas. Evelyn had not been home in a year, and she had lost the knack of dealing with her mother. She sided with her sister in a minor argument, which infuriated her mother, who slapped Evelyn several times and locked her in her childhood room.

All the old feelings of terror and confinement came back to Evelyn, and over the next few weeks back on her job she was so depressed she seldom slept or ate. Then came the second devastating event. Her company experienced major losses in one of its divisions, and the CEO turned to Evelyn's division to bail them out. Evelyn had been a key player in the development of a new product that the CEO decided should be brought to market right away. For five weeks Evelyn worked nearly around the clock.

The intensity of the work kept her mind off her troubles, but when the project was suddenly aborted because a competing firm brought out a similar piece of equipment, Evelyn fell apart. Following a failed suicide attempt with some pills, she ended up in the hospital.

Unfortunately, her saga is far from unique. The Institute of

Living, a psychiatric hospital in Hartford, Connecticut, has an entire ward devoted to the treatment of professionals, many of them baby boomers. An Institute therapist, Hilary Baldwin, MSW, says that most of the patients fit a similar profile. "They're highly ambitious, bright, articulate, and high-functioning, and it's all that that masks the underlying poor sense of self," Baldwin told me. "They can pull it off for several years—the career scene and good salaries, benefits and status. But it's just not enough. They really feel empty inside."

For bright baby boomers from troubled families, work often becomes what psychoanalysts call a *conflict-free zone,* a place where they can function well despite their emotional turmoil. But work can protect them only so long. Eventually they get overtired or overly settled in their professions and the physical or emotional symptoms of a crash begin to surface.

TREVOR'S HAVEN

You need not grow up in a grossly dysfunctional or abusive family, however, to seek refuge in a profession. Most of the prematurely foreclosed women and men I met had run away from domestic circumstances far less ghastly than what Evelyn faced. Their parents' afflictions were the familiar ones of the 1950s and 1960s—mothers who were angry or depressed and fathers who were absent.

Asked how he decided at the tender age of thirteen to become an accountant, Trevor Mason, forty-four, of Rochester, New York, told me, "My seventh-grade algebra teacher, who was a father figure for me, had been an accountant before he went into teaching. When he'd talk about the profession, it sounded very orderly and methodical, and order was something I desperately craved, because I didn't have much of it in my home life."

Trevor explained that when he was ten years old, his mother

moved him and his older brother halfway around the globe from Melbourne, Australia, where he was born, to Atlanta, Georgia, where his mother had grown up. Trevor's father, a dentist, had dumped her in favor of his nineteen-year-old hygienist, and his mother decided to camp out at her parents' house until she could get her life back in order.

In the seven years between the family's emigration to America and Trevor's entering college, his mother, who had never intended to work outside the home, went through a series of secretarial jobs she detested. She also had several love affairs and married a salesman whose company promptly relocated him, his new wife, and his two stepsons first to Miami and later to St. Louis.

Trevor's brother refused to come along for the Missouri move. Instead he dropped out of high school, got a job with a Miami construction company, and rented an apartment of his own.

"I had the opposite reaction, I got *more* involved with my schoolwork," Trevor recounted. "I got straight A's that first year in Miami, and I became treasurer of the student government even though I was only a sophomore.

"I just really latched on to this idea of myself as a budding young accountant. The other kids thought I was the biggest nerd they'd ever seen."

The turbulence of his youth accounts also, Trevor suggested, for why, later in life, he remained in a job long after he stopped enjoying the work. Even after the job began to make him physically ill he continued with it.

During the mid-1980s, after Trevor had been employed in one of the photographic film divisions at Kodak for nearly two decades, the company drastically reduced its staff. Trevor's workload doubled as a result, a pet project he had counted on to propel him into the executive ranks got canceled, and he developed headaches his doctor identified as job-related.

The headaches worsened over the following year to the point where on some days Trevor couldn't focus well enough to drive. Yet rather than go out and look for another job, he simply increased the doses of pain medication he consumed.

"I honestly could not see where I had any choice but to continue at Kodak," said Trevor. "Security and stability are more important to me than to a lot of people because of what I experienced as a kid. And given that I was in my forties and had been with the same company my whole career, I wasn't a strong contender for a position with another firm.

"Besides," he added, "even if I found another position somewhere, I couldn't see where I would gain anything. I'd be doing the same work, after all."

The possibility of doing something different—putting his skills to use in another branch of accounting or retraining for a new profession—never even crossed his mind, Trevor said when we spoke eighteen months after he finally did leave Kodak.

For someone who prematurely foreclosed his options in childhood, the notion of having options is hard to grasp. Having followed a single course since childhood, such a person doesn't know how to think about alternatives. Unlike those of us who recall from adolescence the joy of experimenting with diverse visions of ourselves, a prematurely foreclosed baby boomer has little or no experience searching out and trying on vocations and lifestyles.

In Trevor's case, it virtually took an engraved invitation to make him consider breaking out. One morning an assistant to the head of his division came around and personally delivered information kits about an early retirement package Kodak was offering. Targeted primarily at employees in their fifties and sixties, the program also welcomed younger managers who had been with the company ten years or more.

When Trevor brought the materials home and showed them

to his wife, she urged him to sign on. Worried about his health, she had a selfish reason as well for wanting him to quit. The interior design business she had started several years earlier had suddenly taken off and needed a financial manager.

"She has a knack for matching colors and selling her services to wealthy women, but not for balancing books," said Trevor, who has divided his time since he quit between his wife's business and his own concerns.

Like every other prematurely foreclosed baby boomer I interviewed who had jumped ship, Trevor said he found he needs some time for self-exploration before he can commit to a new work routine. A couple of months after leaving Kodak, he took a three-week trip to Australia where he held tearful reunions with his father, whom he hadn't seen in more than thirty years, and with aunts, uncles, and cousins he barely remembered.

More recently, he's been absorbed with the possibility of returning to school and tooling up for another vocation. He is afflicted, though, with a disability that commonly strikes prematurely foreclosed men and women who leave their old careers. Once they finally open themselves up to new possibilities, they find it hard to focus down.

"I find myself interested in *everything*," Trevor confided. At the time we met, he was taking classes part-time at the University of Rochester in marketing, computer science, and advertising. "Soon," he said, "I'm going to have to give myself a deadline for making up my mind, but so far, I don't feel ready. I'm having too much fun."

HER MOTHER'S SHINING STAR

Another group of baby boomers internalized their parents' frustrations with their own careers—or lack of careers, in the case of their mothers—and unconsciously set out to make it up to them by their own choice of work. For the past twenty or thirty years, these boomers have been acting in their parents' stead.

Susan Turvey, forty-three, a former lawyer, made a comment during our interview that I heard frequently from other women. "My mother was overeducated for her position in life," said Susan. "Because of the times she grew up in, and because she had children early, she didn't get to live out her potential. In many ways I lived out her ambitions. She was so unhappy, I felt my role in this world was to make my mother happy by living out her unfulfilled fantasies."

The fact that mothers of baby boomers frequently conveyed to their daughters their dissatisfaction at being homemakers or caught up in low-status jobs is well documented. In one study, fully two thirds of mothers had talked with their daughters about unfulfilled career aspirations they had.

Studies show, too, the considerable impact that these mothers' ambitions had on their female offspring. Whether or not the mothers themselves worked outside the home, if they wanted their daughters to have careers, that desire had an enormous influence.

In a gender reversal on the age-old story of the son who makes good on his impoverished father's dreams, scores of baby boomer daughters set out to do what their mothers could only imagine. But the results, even for those who did well, sometimes have been less than rewarding. Some daughters ended up in jobs that didn't suit them and in relationships with their mothers where they were unable to separate and become their own person.

Susan Turvey and her mother are a case in point. Valedictorian of her high school class in Indianapolis, Phi Beta Kappa at Swarthmore, an editor of *Law Review* at Yale, Susan endured exhaustion and indignity to become the second woman partner in her prestigious New York City law firm. Given assignments twice as demanding as those her male counterparts worked on, she also had to contend with a senior partner who several times came into her office, closed the door, and propositioned her. His response to her rebuffs was a concerted and successful campaign against her candidacy for partnership. On the first vote, she was turned down.

When Susan fought the decision, the partners eventually caved in, but only after a hellish, fourteen-month-long battle during which her boyfriend moved out and her oldest, closest friend became highly critical of her for not moving on. This friend, a lawyer herself, advised Susan to stop being masochistic and take a job at any of a dozen other good firms in town.

It was her mother, Susan said, who pulled her through. She moved into Susan's apartment for several weeks and provided cooking, cleaning, and consolation. "I used to tell people that Mom acted like it was *her* fight, like she was the one who'd been mistreated," Susan recalled.

Once the partnership battle was finally won, Susan felt elated. For the better part of a year, she did nothing but celebrate. First she went on a monthlong vacation, hiking and skiing in the Rocky Mountains. Then, when she returned, she bought an apartment on Fifth Avenue, which her mother helped her decorate. At the office, she made a secret deal with a couple of the women paralegals and several secretaries to keep diaries of abusive remarks made by the partner who had opposed her.

But once Susan had settled into her new life, things unexpectedly changed. Despite the fact that she considered herself a hardened New Yorker, she couldn't keep dirt and crime, which hadn't much concerned her when she lived down in SoHo, out of her mind. Susan went around the apartment cleaning soot off the windowsills on days between the twice-weekly visits by the cleaning woman she'd hired.

At her job, too, annoyances she had previously ignored began to drive her crazy. During her partnership struggle, she used to awaken at dawn feeling anxious and angry, yet geared up to go out and prove herself. Now she found herself waking up anxious and angry once again, but loath to leave her bed for another day of meetings with partners she detested and clients she considered overly demanding.

Her mother's reaction during this period also disappointed Susan. While once her mother had fought beside her, now she no longer seemed willing even to hear about Susan's troubles. "It was as if my life, which had been an exciting drama for her for several years, suddenly became very boring," Susan remembers.

THE FAMILY HERO

To therapists who treat high achievers, Susan's predicament is familiar. "It gets harder and harder to be in the role of family hero," says Joan Burns, Ph.D., a psychologist in Birmingham, Alabama. "No matter how hard people try, they can't pull it off anymore. They can't continue to hide their own problems or be fantastic enough in their performance to surmount the problems of the parents they are trying to be a star for."

Susan herself, after her depression deepened to the point she stopped eating properly and lost interest in seeing friends, consulted a therapist. When I asked her what insights she gained there, she responded, "I'd created a life that was not really my own, but my mother's." Not only did she have the kind of professional career that her mother's straight A's and ambitions in college should have afforded her, Susan explained, she was living in the city where her mother had always dreamed of living, in an apartment decorated in her mother's style.

To move from that initial realization to engineering a life of her own choosing has not been easy, however. Susan went through a long period of hating first her mother, then her therapist, and feeling all the more stuck and alone.

Susan recalled for me a series of conversations she eventually had with her therapist that propelled her out of her rut. The pivotal point came in the middle of a session when she told the therapist she "felt like a tourist" in both the legal field and in New York.

"Where *do* you feel at home?" the therapist asked.

"On a mountain trail in Colorado," Susan answered, half joking, remembering how contented she had been while on vacation.

The therapist immediately remarked, "Perhaps the National Park Service needs an attorney."

For reasons Susan did not fully understand at first, the remark angered her. She had just spent several weeks detailing how much she hated the law. And her hope had been that if she complained enough, her therapist would eventually *order* her to change careers. In fact, she'd fantasized that the therapist would even prescribe which alternative field she ought to pursue. Then Susan could quit her firm with no guilt or ambivalence.

When instead the therapist suggested she join the National Park Service, the remark struck Susan as mocking. Only after several additional therapy sessions did Susan come to appreciate that her therapist was being neither cruel nor disingenuous. She was merely trying to impress upon Susan the breadth of opportunities available to her.

There are big rewards for prematurely foreclosed baby boomers who find a way to cut themselves some slack. When they break out of their old molds, these people often become, in the words of another of my interviewees, "like middle-aged teenagers." Feeling liberated and venturesome, they explore whole new places, vocations, and ways of living.

In the half-dozen years since Susan resigned from her law firm, she has done legal work for a consumer agency in New York, fund-raising for a foundation in Boston, and served as an admissions officer for her alma mater, Swarthmore, where she chose to live in a student dormitory. At the time I met her, she was in her eleventh month as director of a large charitable foundation in Seattle and had bought a six-unit apartment building, the top floor of which she occupies herself.

"Some of America's most gorgeous hiking trails are within an hour's drive," replied Susan when asked why she chose to move to Seattle, "and the men here aren't bad-looking either."

She expects to stay in Seattle for a long while, Susan said. The city is large enough to have good restaurants and theater and far enough from Indianapolis that her mother will seldom visit.

Considering how much better off she is now, why did Susan wait until she was in her forties to get to this point? What kept her from readjusting her relationship with her mother ten or twenty years earlier?

The simplest answer is that she was too busy making a success in her profession. But there's another, less obvious, reason as well. Both Susan and her mother derived real benefits from their tangled tie to each other and thus had good reason to perpetuate it.

Susan's mother was able to postpone indefinitely the feelings of abandonment that accompany a child's leaving home. Mrs. Turvey was the only mom in the women's dormitory at Swarthmore who didn't cry as she kissed her daughter good-bye on the first day of freshman year. "The other moms pitied themselves their empty nests," Susan recollected. "But my mother acted as if she'd been given front-row seats at the World Series or something. She treated my college and law school years like a spectator sport. We talked almost every day, and she cheered me on and celebrated each of my little victories."

Susan had cause to feel fortunate, too. "My friends who didn't get along with their mothers were forever saying they envied the way I could confide in her and count on her to be there," she relayed, adding that she's slowly rebuilding a relationship with her mother via telephone.

CROSSOVER DREAMS

I also interviewed women and men who chased the dreams not of their same-sex parent, but the parent of the *opposite* sex. Their motivation for prematurely foreclosing their options was no different from Susan Turvey's, Trevor Mason's, or Evelyn Breen's. They were trying to save themselves from the frightening fate they felt sure awaited them.

"I was terrified of turning out like my dad," said Rob Pellegrini, thirty-four, in accounting for his decision at age twelve to become a novelist. "My dad was a highly paid scientist with DuPont, but he had no life. He'd arrive home late every night in a bad mood, mix himself a stiff drink, eat reheated leftovers, growl at us kids for half an hour, then stare at the TV until he nodded off in his easy chair."

Rob's mother, by contrast, is a writer who has never made much money but "has about as close to an ideal existence as a human can get," according to her son. Virtually every weekday for as far back as Rob can remember, she's gone off to her study at 9 A.M. and worked on her novels until noon, at which time she reemerges for lunch, then drives to the local college where for many years she took courses toward her bachelor's and master's degrees and more recently has been teaching creative writing courses part-time.

Unfortunately, Rob's own life as a writer has not proven so idyllic. In fact, at the age of twenty-eight he gave up on writing and took a job managing a bookstore in Atlanta.

Rob and his wife had moved to Atlanta after he graduated from the master's degree program in creative writing at Syracuse University. A year later, when Rob was only twenty-five, he had his first novel published by a major publishing house. But he quickly discovered he couldn't make ends meet. "The reason I abandoned my writing career," said Rob, "can be summed in one word—money. I made a whopping five thousand bucks off my first novel, and my literary agent couldn't get me any more than that for my second.

"I had a wife and daughter to support, and I felt horribly guilty. My wife was working overtime at a job she didn't like in order to keep the family fed, and I couldn't let her go on doing that indefinitely."

In other words, it wasn't just money but also his gender role that caused Rob to crash. If as a boy he was able to elect his mother as his vocational role model, as a man he could not continue to follow her lead. He couldn't live off his spouse indefinitely the way his mother had lived off his father. Although gender roles have evolved over the past few decades, they have not reversed themselves.

"It's a frustrating situation," Rob said. "I'd rather be writing novels than selling copies of other authors', but I can't cop out on my family obligations. Unless your name is John Updike or Joseph Heller, it's not realistic to expect to make a living as a serious novelist."

WHEN FATHERS AND DAUGHTERS COMPETE

Women who prematurely choose their fathers' professions face roughly the reverse of Rob's dilemma. As young adults they come to feel they mustn't be overly successful lest they overshadow the key males in their lives, their fathers in particular.

Only in recent times have many daughters had the option of identifying with their fathers' vocational interests, and in some families the potential payoffs for doing so are great. By opting into her father's profession from an early age, a daughter has the chance to become her father's compatriot and favored child. And out in the larger world, as she makes her way into occupations populated mostly by men, she has what many other women do not: a dependable male mentor.

Her father benefits as well. He enjoys being admired and respected by her, and he shares in her accomplishments. He may even avert the possibility of losing her to other men. In an update on the medieval practice of locking daughters in their rooms when suitors arrived, some fathers keep their daughters so tied up preparing for careers that the daughters have little chance to fall in love and marry.

But if a daughter grows up and begins to exceed her father's accomplishments in his own profession, the whole arrangement may fall apart. The daughter ceases to be her father's protégée and becomes instead a potential threat to his male ego, or even a competitor within his professional world.

The problem arises for daughters who've been chasing dreams that their fathers never achieved. On the verge of great success, these women find themselves curiously immobilized. Said Laurie Bartkowski, thirty-three, of Washington, D.C., in explaining why she has become unable to finish her doctoral dissertation: "It would be a betrayal of my father in a way to get my Ph.D. and a good job. To finish my degree would mean to succeed where my father failed."

Laurie's father, the son of Polish immigrants, was the pride of his extended family as a young man. After graduating valedictorian of his high school class, he went to Yale as an undergraduate, and on to the University of Chicago for graduate work. But for reasons still unclear to Laurie, he never completed his doctorate, and for the past thirty years he has taught art history in a community college.

Still, it was her father who tracked Laurie into academia practically from the day she was born. "He drummed into me the distinction between what he called 'the real world' and the world of arts and ideas, a clearly superior world where he lived and where I was meant to reside," recalled Laurie, an only child whose mother died when she was in first grade.

Laurie recounted an evening two years later, when she was eight years old and made plans to get together with Becky Ritchie, "the coolest girl in the third grade." Becky had volunteered to come over and teach Laurie how to make book covers out of brown paper bags, but Laurie's father objected.

"Other kids learned from their parents how to make book covers, but that sort of activity was way too pedestrian for my father," said Laurie. "I remember when I said to my dad, 'Becky's going to come over tonight after supper,' and he said, 'No, dear, I don't think I could bear any aliens in the house tonight.' All kids were aliens in my father's eyes if they were normal children who did the things normal children do."

Not that her father was *mean*, Laurie hastened to add. He could be very comforting, in fact. One day in kindergarten a couple of kids called her names and shoved her around, and that night she had a nightmare in which the kids who picked on her were transformed into monsters. When she woke up terrified and crying, her father, hearing her screams, came to Laurie's room and rocked her in his arms until she stopped crying. Then he led her by flashlight downstairs to his study, where he put a recording of a Brahms piano concerto on the stereo and read a Dr. Seuss story to her until she fell asleep on his lap.

Laurie recollected several other episodes of a similar sort from her childhood. In each instance, when she ventured into the world of her peers, and was hurt or insulted, her father brought her back to his safe haven of books and music.

When Laurie announced at about age ten or eleven that she wanted to be an English teacher when she grew up, her father was thrilled. He grew ever more so as she progressed through high school and college with straight A's and was accepted into a half-dozen top-ranked doctoral programs around the country.

Turning down places like Harvard and Stanford, Laurie selected for her graduate studies the Department of English at Duke University. Big-name professors in post-structuralism—the hot theory at that point in 1986—were on the faculty there, and the graduate seminars crackled with intellectual electricity. Faculty and students believed they were reshaping the way literature would be studied for decades to come.

Laurie was a star student in the Duke program, and her troubles did not begin until she was well into work on her doctoral dissertation, five years after she began her graduate training. Having completed all of her course work, defended her dissertation proposal, and gathered the materials to write her dissertation, she became blocked. All the ideas were there, yet after a full year of work, she had barely completed half a chapter.

During the same year, Laurie's financial fellowship expired and she had to scramble for money to support herself. For a semester she taught freshman composition courses, and then, feeling tired and disaffected, she decided to take a leave of absence and depart Duke for a while.

At the time, Laurie believed her move was motivated primarily by economic concerns. When she took out a calculator and divided her salary as an instructor by the hours she spent marking students' papers and meeting with them, she discovered her rate of pay came out just above minimum wage. So when a fellow English student told her about a job he could help her get, writing speeches for a Democratic candidate, she jumped at the chance.

"I thought, I'll do this for six or eight months, then return to Durham refreshed and ready to write," Laurie told me a half year into her stay in Washington. "But now I'm no longer certain just where I belong. Do I really want to spend the rest of my days sequestered in an ivy-covered building in a college town somewhere out in the sticks? The real world of politics is a lot less solitary and precious. On the other hand, it can be very crude and unimaginative."

Noting that this impossible opposition of "the real world" and the academy is one she learned from her father, Laurie said he continues to make it hard for her to commit to one option or the other. When they talk by phone, he urges her to stay in his world, while at the same time sending her the message she shouldn't do so in a way that would outdo his own accomplishments. In one breath he warns her of the crassness of politics, and in the next he reassures her that it's okay to turn in a less than excellent dissertation, even if that means she doesn't get a job at a major university.

With the help of a therapist she's been consulting, Laurie has begun to appreciate how intricately woven is the spider web in which she trapped herself when she prematurely foreclosed her options. "Sometimes I get angry and want to just reject what he's saying, and him along with it, like a rebellious teenager," she said, acknowledging a need people often have at midlife if they overconformed as adolescents.

"But to do that is to fall under his sway as completely as if I entirely accept his point of view," Laurie rightly noted. "Either way I'm reacting to him rather than choosing for myself."

She added an observation that every prematurely foreclosed baby boomer sooner or later comes to appreciate. "The only way to really break free," said Laurie, "is to look at my options in different ways than my father does. It sounds odd for a thirty-three-year-old woman to say this, but I have to figure out what it means to *me* to stay with academia or give it up, irrespective of my father's interests."

CHAPTER 6

THE REBEL AT
MIDLIFE

Crashes frequently serve as overdue notices that something remains unresolved in a baby boomer's life. That unfinished business may date back all the way to childhood, as in the case of the prematurely foreclosed, or to adolescence.

For one key group of baby boomers, the root cause of career crashes is a set of political and philosophical commitments they made while in high school or college. These are the rebels who came of age in the 1960s and participated in the protest and countercultural movements of that era. As adults, their lives differ in important ways from other boomers their age. As a group, they make less money, have smaller families, and are more liberal in their political views. They also tend to work not in corporate settings but either in "helping professions" such as social work and medicine, or as artists, writers, or teachers.

Unlike many other people who crash, their problem is not that they have lost respect for themselves or the work they do. Nor have they embraced the work ethic of the 1990s, in which individuals put their own wants and needs above those of the organizations that employ them. On the contrary, rebels crash under the weight of their own devotion to a set of values that at midlife, and especially in the current economic climate, have become virtually untenable.

Chronically dismayed over how little money they make and how little respect they get from the clients they serve, they feel cornered. They fantasize doing what so many of their former comrades have done: give up on the impoverished inner-city schools where they teach and go to work in the suburbs, quit their jobs at the family clinics, and open up private counseling practices. But before they can take the plunge, they're stopped short by guilt, certain they're selfishly abandoning people who will not be served if they leave.

Rebels themselves report feeling left behind by their peers. "On a very deep level they still want to make their lives count by all the definitions they set up more than twenty years ago," says Mary Lynne Musgrove, a career adviser in Columbus, Ohio. "But they no longer feel the companionship of others who want to do that. Everybody else seems to have climbed off the train."

Little wonder they have that impression. Anyone who reads newspapers or watches television has heard, over the past fifteen years, how rebels from the 1960s transformed themselves into yuppies. Following the lead of Jerry Rubin, the story goes, they donned suits and took up practice on Wall Street.

In point of fact, although many rebels have joined the mainstream, many others have not. Social scientists who study the lives of dissidents from the 1960s report that no mass conversion has taken place. In spite of what the general public (and many rebels) have been led to believe, thousands of baby boomers continue to practice at midlife what they preached in their rebellious youth.

Sociologists Jack Whalen and Richard Flacks, who have systematically tracked former campus activists over the past quarter century, confirm that most still subscribe to the code of ethics they adopted in college. That code consists of four major tenets, summarized by Whalen and Flacks in their book *Beyond the Barricades: The Sixties Generation Grows Up:* don't work for a defense contractor; don't work for a multinational corporation; don't work for a company that pollutes the environment; and live your life so that you are not part of the problem.

WHAT MAKES DEBORAH STAY

Deborah Solomon, forty-three, has spent half her life staunchly living up to those principles. She is the executive director of the Safe Home Association, an organization in Denver that had a paid staff of eight at its peak in the early 1980s but has shrunk down to just Deborah and a handful of volunteers.

A leader in Students for a Democratic Society (SDS) while a student at the University of Colorado in the late 1960s, Deborah worked after graduation in peace groups until the Vietnam War came to an end, then shifted her energies to women's issues. One night in 1974, while finishing some paperwork at the Denver Women's Center, she became involved for the first time with the plight of abused wives.

At 11 P.M. the telephone rang, and the woman on the other end spoke so quietly Deborah could barely make out her words. She said she was calling on a phone she'd taken into the bathroom so her husband wouldn't hear. "She'd been battered and terrorized," Deborah recalled, "and at that time there was no movement to protect battered women. The listing for the Women's Center was the nearest thing she could find."

The caller said her husband had hit her several times. She was bleeding from her nose and mouth and didn't know what to do. If she stayed in the house he'd beat her again, but she didn't dare inform the neighbors of what had happened.

Knowing she had to help somehow, Deborah got the woman's address, urged her to sneak out of the house, and drove out and picked her up. As they were driving away the husband ran after Deborah's car.

When she got the woman to the Center, she set up a makeshift bed from sofa cushions and a sleeping bag, and throughout most of the night Deborah listened to her horror stories and tried to comfort her. First thing the next morning, Deborah called around to social agencies in search of one that could help.

But before she could find one, the woman panicked and returned home. As she walked out, she thanked Deborah for her kindness and asked her not to notify the police.

Over the following weeks, Deborah read everything she could find on family violence and located the few people around Denver charged with countering the problem. One of them, an administrator in a welfare office, created a part-time, minimum-wage position for Deborah to help battered women find temporary housing.

In the twenty months she stayed at that job, she developed a network of social workers, activists, and battered women, and together they started a nonprofit organization they called the Safe Home Association. As a result in part of good timing (wife abuse became a national issue in the late 1970s), but mostly of Deborah's own persistence, the organization succeeded. She gave speeches, organized rallies, and wrote grant proposals—efforts that produced enough money to fund four shelters, underwrite an educational program in the public schools, and pay Deborah a modest salary.

But then came the 1980s and Ronald Reagan's presidency. With every year that passed, federal funding for social programs decreased. State and local governments, already strapped, diverted more and more of their own resources to keep schools, parks, and prisons open. For the SHA to survive, its leaders had to turn to private charities, and in particular, to conventional women's clubs like the Junior League, which Deborah reviles as "playpens for pampered wives of the corporate elite."

By 1987 or 1988, Deborah had grown so discouraged that on nights before she had to dress up in expensive clothes and beg for money from people she didn't respect, she would drink herself to sleep. Her speeches, impassioned in the early years, began to sound mechanical.

"I hit bottom," Deborah recollected. "I wasn't eating or sleeping very much, and one night, at a dinner with some potential donors, I got really smashed. I practically totaled my car on the way home."

Fortunately, the judge who tried her on DWI charges was someone she had advised on several difficult child custody cases over the years. "He could have thrown the book at me, but instead he sent me to AA, which was a lifesaver," she said. Not only did Deborah find sobriety in Alcoholics Anonymous, she got together with the man who is now her husband. An attorney who had been volunteering his time to the SHA for several years, he was someone she never imagined was a recovering alcoholic.

Deborah also credits AA with what she terms her "artistic awakening." Following the lead of fellow members who had exchanged inebriated nights in barrooms for evening courses at local colleges, she signed up for a twice-a-week painting class. There she discovered, to her surprise, that she had real talent. A couple of her early pieces were so good, in fact, the teacher showed them to the owner of an art gallery, who took them on consignment.

"I wish," Deborah admitted, "I could paint full-time and give up the SHA. My heart is really in my studio these days. I can't muster up the enthusiasm to resuscitate this place anymore."

Hers is not just a vain wish. Unlike most would-be artists, Deborah has reason to believe she could make more money from her art than in her current job. Having won prizes in several juried shows, she has sold her paintings for good prices and had offers to do assignment work for office buildings. The way Deborah and her husband figure it, she'd have little trouble surpassing the $23,000 she paid herself out of the dwindling SHA budget.

Deborah's husband strongly urged her, in fact, to make the move. Concerned by how demoralized she was each evening when she returned home, he made her a proposal a few months prior to the day she and I met. He offered to take on a few high-priced matrimonial cases over the following year so she could better equip her studio and not worry about their cash flow.

At first Deborah was delighted by her husband's proposal. "It was as if he had offered to release me from a straitjacket I'd been in," she recalled. "I had reached a point where I felt like, 'I'm worth more than what it takes to keep this organization alive, I've done what I can do and I'm tired.'"

Nonetheless, she has not been able to move onward. "I just can't abandon the women we help. The organization may not survive if I stay, but it *definitely* will die if I leave.

"Besides," she said, "the more I've thought about relying on my husband, even partially, the more it bothers me. The money would be coming from some wealthy woman's divorce settlement. It flys in the face of all my values."

Deborah feels hemmed in, unable to embrace either of the usual remedies for a career crash, revitalizing a job or switching out of it. Nor do the pleasures of painting compensate her for her frustrations at work. "You can't do good creative work when you're depressed and distracted," she attested. "I haven't painted anything I'm proud of in a long while."

COMPROMISED BY THEIR VALUES

Richard Horevitz, Ph.D., a psychologist who has counseled many activists, says that those who try to be what he refers to as "all-purpose moms or saviors" only do damage to themselves and their causes. "They let everybody dump everything on them, and in the end, they're not helping anybody," he told me when we spoke at his office on Michigan Avenue in Chicago.

Horevitz became aware of this martyr syndrome in the early 1980s when several baby boomer physicians who work in the same hospital began coming to him for help. They showed up separately at his office but displayed similar emotional problems. They were all on the staff at Cook County Hospital, and they all complained of exhaustion, depression, anxiety, and wrecked relationships.

These politically committed doctors had been attracted to Cook County back in the late 1960s and the 1970s because it was one of the nation's largest hospitals serving poor inner-city residents, and also because its leaders enacted an egalitarian form of administration. Nurses, interns, and nonmedical staff played dominant roles in setting policy within the hospital.

One unintended result, however, was workloads that were nothing short of inhuman. On top of all the physical and emotional challenges that confront any physician at an over-crowded, understaffed hospital in a crime-ridden neighborhood, these physicians had additional burdens. As Horevitz observes, "In a system where everybody is empowered, people are always having meetings and fighting for power." Besides their clinical duties, doctors at Cook County were called upon to attend endless grievance hearings, union negotiations, and committee gatherings.

When they showed up at Horevitz's office, they had little to show for the ten or twenty years they put into the hospital. Too taxed to maintain relationships, they lived alone or in troubled marriages. Their incomes were half to a third of what their fellow physicians made in private practice. And they harbored serious doubts about whether their sacrifices produced much tangible good. Suspecting that the level of patient care at Cook County was little better than at other urban hospitals, they also doubted the support staff was happier.

Yet, reports Horevitz, for all their discouragement, these physicians were not ready to seek greener pastures. If he tried to suggest they consider alternative career options, they gave him a dozen good reason why they should stay at Cook County. "Psychotherapy with them is different from psychotherapy with the garden-variety patient who is chronically unhappy," Horevitz notes. "They are like seventeenth-century Jesuits or Talmudic scholars. They're highly dedicated, and they've already spent twenty years engaged in values clarification at 'rap meetings' and in political groups they belong to."

The kinds of soul-searching conventional professionals do for the first time during career crashes, rebel professionals have done incessantly. If anything, they've asked themselves too often about the larger meaning and worth of their life's work.

"Survivors of the 1960s make themselves subservient to their values. The values don't guide them, they drive them," Horevitz says. "To thrive in their middle years, they have to reformulate their lives so that their political values are in line with their personal values."

In practice, what that's usually meant for Horevitz's physician-patients is to locate new jobs where they can help people they care about, reserve time for themselves and their families, and still stay clear of corporate medicine. Some go to work for health maintenance organizations. Others start private practices in which they devote a substantial percentage of their time to Medicare, Medicaid, or noninsured patients. And some get out of direct patient care altogether in favor of government jobs where they help formulate public health policies.

MICHELLE: A REBEL WITHOUT A CACHE

Sad to say, many baby boomers who have stayed the course they set for themselves in adolescence do not have such rosy alternatives available to them. Some work in fields where jobs are scarce. Others lack credentials. Still others never even settled into a profession in the first place. The very notion of a career, no matter how noble, was anathema to them.

"The youth revolt of the sixties embodied two rather contradictory perspectives on self-development and transformation," write sociologists Jack Whalen and Richard Flacks. One perspective, that of the political activists, called for "active involvement in public events" and "continuous examination of one's duty to take action." By contrast, the other perspective, which grew out of the counterculture, emphasized "the personal rather than the political, retreatism rather than revolutionary action."

Counterculturalists dedicated themselves to the pursuit of alternative lifestyles, to living, as Whalen and Flacks characterized it, "freely, expressively, and fully." The counterculturalists' goal in life was not to save the world but to extricate themselves from the mainstream. Instead of going into fields like medicine, teaching, or social work, which require set work hours and established protocols, they have worked as free-lance writers and artists, or in alternative bookstores and food co-ops. They maintain what Michelle LaCroix, a woman in Boston, called "a rigid determination never to do work that doesn't feed me spiritually."

The ultimate dissenters of the baby boom generation, counterculturalists lived quietly on the margins of American society throughout the 1970s and 1980s. But in recent years they've found it tougher to survive at the edge. In the neighborhoods they used to populate—SoHo and Greenwich Village in New York, Uptown in Chicago, the Mission District in San Francisco—one-bedroom apartments rent for $1,000 a month or more, if you can find one that hasn't gone condo. And in rustic hideaways such as Woodstock, New York, and Big Sur, California, which tourist guides still describe as hippie havens, housing sells in the $250,000 to $1 million range.

Age is also a problem for counterculturalists. By thirty-five or forty-five, almost anyone grows tired of being unsettled. "I feel like I'll never get my act together," lamented Michelle LaCroix, who is forty-four. "Here I am, a middle-aged, college-educated woman about to go beg for another minimum-wage job."

At the time she and I spoke in a Boston coffee shop, Michelle's half-time job as an art teacher at a community center was about to come to an end, and her roommate had moved out. Within weeks of our interview she would have to choose between living on the streets, imposing herself on friends, or moving in with her parents in New Jersey.

That last option Michelle had taken a few years earlier during another crash. When the fringe art gallery where she worked went broke, she fell behind in rent payments and was evicted. Having to turn to her folks for refuge was degrading, Michelle said, but in her dejected frame of mind, it also seemed oddly appropriate—a perverse poetic justice.

"Most people by age forty have homes and families and occupations. I had nothing. The one thing I could vaguely call my own—my apartment—was taken away from me too, and I crawled back home to mommy and daddy."

For eight months she ate junk food, watched television, and bickered with her parents. "I swore when it was over," she relayed, "that I'd die before I'd let that happen to me again."

To pull herself out of that earlier crash, Michelle made a

choice that in her twenties she would never even have considered. She took a job in the advertising department of a large corporation. "I was sick of being poor, and I thought it was high time I got some return on my graphic arts degree."

Since graduating from New York University in 1969, she has turned down opportunities for jobs in advertising agencies several times, opting instead to make what money she could designing experimental arts magazines and promoting alternative galleries. Periodically during those two decades she also left Boston for a year or two to live on communes or in arts colonies.

Although Michelle was instantly unhappy at the corporate job she took in 1988, she stayed long enough to be eligible for unemployment benefits and accumulate money for a down payment on a two-bedroom apartment in South Boston. Then she got herself fired. In the eighteen months between then and when I met her, she had returned to her old lifestyle, which she's paid for by taking assorted part-time jobs and renting out her second bedroom.

But as Michelle contemplated going out to look for yet another poorly paid arts job, she showed all the classic signs of someone in the midst of a crash. Depressed and isolated, she blamed herself for the predicament she was in.

"What kind of adult in her mid-forties," Michelle asked, "doesn't even have her own savings account?

"I'm not saying I wish I had been a lawyer and had two-point-five children and a home in Brookline. But you begin to wonder what your life adds up to when you're halfway through it and you can't even manage the payments on a grubby little apartment."

LOOKING ON THE BRIGHT SIDE

According to Terry Kupers, a psychiatrist in Oakland, California, who has specialized in treating counterculturalists, rebels often reproach themselves for their lack of achievement.

"They're bitter that they gave up opportunities when they were young because of their commitments and the commitments didn't get them anywhere," he told me. "They look at younger people who come out of college knowing where they are going, and who pass them by, and they say, 'If I had done that, I could be at such-and-such a level now.' "

Kupers said he counters such feelings by reminding his patients how they got where they are. "If someone is sitting around underemployed because in the 1960s they decided that all this competitive business was crap, they tend to forget why they decided not to join the rat race in the first place. You have to remind them of the reasons they chose not to get on a tenure track or go to law school."

To help his clients feel less sorry for themselves, Kupers tells them about another large group of men and women he treats—people their age with lots of money and as many regrets. These are corporate executives who come to therapy saying they wish they had followed their hearts because if they had become jazz musicians or schoolteachers, they'd certainly be happier.

It's not at all easy, however, for these corporate executives to change direction. Having gone the way their elders led them since they were young, they're only dimly aware of their own true interests and values. They also fear what might happen were their income to drop. Family and friends, who would surely suffer as a result, might desert them.

By contrast, rebels seldom confront either of those dilemmas as they consider charting a new course. Since they have always let their passions be their guide, they don't have to wonder about who they really are or what they enjoy. Nor need they fret about their standard of living slipping very far, given how modestly they live.

What keeps rebels spinning their wheels is an inflated moral standard to which they hold themselves. Said Richard Horevitz, the psychologist in Chicago: "It's difficult for them to accept themselves as simply people. They have to be *good* people."

Both species of rebel, the political activist and the counterculturalist, trip over that distinction. Activists, rather than do something that might be seen as selfish, stick with organizations they'd be better off leaving. Counterculturalists, afraid of selling out, impoverish themselves.

PETER'S NEW PRINCIPLE:
TO SUCCEED IS NOT A SIN

Some rebels have gotten out of those ruts. No longer in self-denying jobs or living situations, yet still faithful to their deeper values, they are very clear about what hung them up in the past. They all point to restrictions they imposed on themselves in their youth, restrictions they clung to long after it was reasonable to do so.

"In high school I took up this hippie philosophy that said, 'I hate people who are competitive, I won't be competitive,'" Peter Ogawa, forty-one, an actor in San Francisco, told me. "I wouldn't even play recreational games. It's only been in the past two or three years that I can play card games with my wife.

"When I was younger," Peter went on, "I *needed* that philosophy. My parents wanted me to be a professional person, a doctor or a lawyer, something like that, and I knew I didn't want to. So I'd get B's and C's when I could have gotten A's, and I would just refuse to compete."

Peter's philosophy, defensive though it was, served him well when he first adopted it. Instead of going into a line of work that didn't suit him, he experimented throughout his early twenties with a variety of occupations, then went into acting, a profession he loves. And his values steered him away from a conventional acting career where he would have been forced to perform in television commercials to pay his rent while waiting to be discovered by Broadway.

Instead he joined the alternative theater movement that has flourished in places like San Francisco, Los Angeles, Minneapolis, and Chicago over the last twenty years. By going that route, Peter has had the chance to perform in some of the most challenging and innovative plays produced in America this century and to work with other actors who share his distaste for "the petty, cutthroat atmosphere that pervades the commercial stage."

Not until his late thirties did Peter confront the negative side of his aversion to competition. His wife, a professor at Berkeley, was tired of being the sole provider the better part of each year while Peter was either out of work entirely or cast in productions that paid what she termed "newspaper boy wages."

For his own part, Peter found himself periodically depressed or angry at his lack of achievement. A highly talented actor who had appeared in dozens of critically acclaimed shows, he hardly ever had a big part and never earned the salary he deserved.

"I just got really disgusted with myself," he recalled during our conversation at a theater where he was rehearsing a play in which he had a starring role. "I was thirty-eight years old, and I was saying to myself, 'I'm going to be forty, and what kind of life do I have?' I never knew when the money was coming, and I felt it was time I grew up."

Peter's distress apparently showed. An acquaintance of his, a director, noticing that Peter was not eating well and had started smoking a lot of pot, urged him to join a men's group he belonged to. The members were mostly from the theater and arts community, and once a week they got together and talked about whatever was on their minds.

At first Peter put him off with a remark about having no interest in beating on drums with Robert Bly. But his friend insisted
the group wasn't like that, and finally Peter agreed to attend a
meeting. To his surprise, he liked what he heard. The participants seemed to have a sense of humor about the problems they
discussed, and by the third meeting, Peter was talking about his
own concerns. He described his frustrations at trying to eke out
a living as an actor, and for the first time, he spoke of the envy he
felt whenever he talked with either of his brothers, one a real estate developer and the other a corporate executive. Not only did
they seem so much happier, they were infinitely wealthier.

Then, at a meeting a couple of months after he joined, Peter
asked the group to react to a big change he was thinking of
making. He was going to quit the theater and sell real estate
with his older brother, a condo tycoon.

The response Peter got from the group took him by surprise.
They knew how emasculated it made him feel to live off his
wife, and how cynical he'd become about his noncareer. Yet no
one spoke up to endorse Peter's plan. Instead they asked him a
lot of questions that made him uncomfortable. "Are you good
at math and finance?" "Won't it seem dull showing people
houses day after day?" "Do you really want to play Willie Loman
in *Death of a Salesman* for the next twenty or thirty years?"

"I felt I'd been ganged up on by a bunch of high school guidance counselors," said Peter. But their point was not lost on him.
If he was going to give up the theater to make money, he'd better
find a line of work where he had some interest and ability.

When Peter went off and made a concerted effort to look into
alternatives, the net result was exactly as several members of his
men's group had predicted. He came to see that it was not his
profession that was holding him back but his approach to it.
Plenty of actors with less talent and experience were working

more than he, and for better pay. The only real difference be-tween him and them was their willingness to go out and hustle.

Peter described in our interview how he eventually got out of his rut: "I figured out I'd been getting in my own way. I was so damn proud of myself that I didn't play politics, I didn't get sucked into the whole competitive game, I didn't suck up to influential peo-ple. It was a point of honor with me to be on the sidelines: 'poor but pure,' one of the guys in my men's group said.

"Finally I just decided, 'I'm going to take control of this thing, goddammit, I'm going to put my credentials out there to work for me.'

"I rewrote my résumé, and when I looked at it, I was flabber-gasted. I thought to myself, 'Look at all the stuff you've done! You *do* have a lot to show for the last fifteen years.' In material terms it doesn't add up to much. I mean, it's not a house in the country, it's not an Oscar, I don't have any of those goods. But I have a wealth of experience."

Without abandoning his commitment to noncommercial the-ater, Peter found ways to assert himself and become a success. He began cultivating people who could get him auditions and befriended directors and producers so they'd choose him over other qualified actors. A few weeks before our interview, he won a major role.

"It's mind-bogglingly simple," said Peter, a childlike inno-cence to his voice. "Most jobs are gotten on the basis of who knows you and who likes you. I used to pooh-pooh that. I used to think, 'You hire the best person.' Well, that's bullshit, and be-liefs like that always used to drag me down.

"Now I feel as light as a helium balloon. It feels good to let go of all that baggage."

CHAPTER 7

ANOTHER
VIETNAM LEGACY

The state police responded swiftly when Kent Lovell's estranged wife phoned them at 5 A.M. Her husband had just called sounding deranged and muttering something about killing himself. The dispatcher sent three patrol cars to the big colonial home in a suburb of Princeton, New Jersey, where Kent had been living alone the past six months.

"I heard the sirens blaring and saw the flashing lights and I became terrified," recalled Kent, a respected neurosurgeon. "I thought I was back in Vietnam in combat and I was going to get killed."

His flashback to the war lasted ten minutes. When he snapped out of it the police were on the front lawn urging him to come out. Hesitantly, he opened the front door and, clad only in pajamas, walked onto the porch in the cold morning air. One of the police officers asked if he would let them drive him to a psychiatric hospital for help, and Kent willingly agreed.

Although Kent's crash is perhaps more dramatic than most, the sequence of events leading up to it is a familiar one to counselors who work with white-collar Vietnam veterans. A man goes about his business for fifteen, twenty, even twenty-five years after his return from Vietnam, seldom talking about the war or showing psychological scars, all the while growing increasingly alienated from his family. Then at some point between his early thirties and late forties he starts abusing alcohol or drugs. For years prior to that time, he may have been drinking to numb himself when he felt anxious or if his thoughts drifted back to the war, but he never let booze wreck his career.

Even after things deteriorate at home and he develops serious alcohol or drug problems, he may manage to hold himself together at work for some months or years—until something sends him off the deep end.

For Kent Lovell, who is forty-five, the critical event occurred while he was running to answer an emergency call. He fell on a wet floor at the hospital, damaged a disk in his back, and was ordered to bed for three months.

Accustomed to a hectic lifestyle, Kent quickly grew bored and depressed at home and got into fights with his wife. The two of them had been drifting apart for a decade or more, and this was the last straw. She resented having to wait on him, and once he was able to go back to work, she took their fourteen-year-old daughter and moved out. Kent, who had been downing a gin-and-tonic or two every evening for several years and three or four after particularly rough days, got to the point after his family departed where he drank himself into a stupor every night.

Then, one night as he was leaving the hospital, Kent took a call to the emergency room. A nineteen-year-old boy had split his head open in a motorcycle accident. Upon his arrival at the hospital, dressed in jeans and an old army jacket, he was still alive. But he died on the operating table.

Alone in the physicians' lounge after conveying the news to

the young man's parents, Kent experienced a flashback to the war. It was the first flashback he had had in the twenty years since he returned from Vietnam. Occasionally in the past he would find himself momentarily disoriented and frightened—at the sound of fireworks on the Fourth of July, or if a helicopter flew overhead. But this time he relived in vivid detail the death of another young man in army clothes.

"The boy was about to leave Vietnam for home," Kent said, "and a few of us had just thrown a celebration dinner for him. We took a swim, and I guess this kid had eaten too much. He vomited and aspirated.

"I didn't have the proper equipment to revive him," added Kent, who was a medic during the war. "I felt horribly guilty. In two days' time he would have gone home to his wife and family. When that kid died at the hospital, I just relived the whole thing again. I was back in Vietnam pulling that soldier out of the water, trying to pump air into his mouth."

The flashback seemed to last for hours, although Kent said he was in a trance no longer than fifteen minutes. Once it ended, he got himself together well enough to drive home and drink himself to sleep.

That night, and for the next few, he had ghastly nightmares about Vietnam. The morning when he called his wife at 5 A.M., he had spent much of the night in the bathroom vomiting. Filled with despair at having wrecked his marriage and his relationship with his daughter, he called his wife to plead for another chance.

When the police cars showed up outside the house, the commotion prompted a flashback to one of his first days in Vietnam when the Vietcong ambushed the camp where he was working and he thought for certain he would be killed. "Flashbacks are as scary, if not more so, than the events themselves," Kent told me.

KEEPING POSTTRAUMATIC STRESS AT BAY

Kent spent a full month in the psychiatric hospital. During that time his dreams and flashbacks subsided and he was well on his way to recovery, having entered marital counseling with his wife and joined a Vietnam veterans "rap group" and a chapter of Alcoholics Anonymous.

Unknowingly, Kent had been suffering for some time from posttraumatic stress disorder (PTSD), a condition whose symptoms include feelings of estrangement from others, sleep disturbances, pessimism about the future, and in its more acute phases, dreams or flashbacks of traumatic events.

Other survivors, including concentration camp victims and people whose communities are devastated by floods or fires, also experience PTSD, but at present, most sufferers are Vietnam veterans. More than one fourth of Vietnam veterans— 829,000 people—exhibit PTSD. The vast majority are baby boomers born between the mid-1940s and early 1950s, and not surprisingly, most all are men.

Contrary to popular myth, only a small percentage of PTSD victims are homeless drug addicts or violent criminals. Typically, they have jobs and families. Thousands hold managerial and professional positions.

Although stressful events at work are a common trigger of episodes of PTSD, some veterans susceptible to the disorder have kept the symptoms at bay for decades while working in high-pressure jobs. Well-off Vietnam veterans—attorneys, physicians, and corporate managers and executives—have been especially adept at evading symptoms, according to counselors who work with them.

Often these men deploy a combination of intense workaholism and mild alcoholism to stave off PTSD. Explained Jerry Melnyk, a counselor at the West Los Angeles Vet Center: "They work sixty hours a week. They're immersed in their work with the same intensity they had in combat in Vietnam. That is their way of coping. When they go home, they drink to get to sleep and keep the bad dreams away."

One man, a senior manager at TRW, recalled a period several years earlier when he had routinely stayed at the office sixteen to eighteen hours a day and had taken amphetamines to stay awake. "I couldn't stand to go to sleep," he told me. "I knew I'd have this awful nightmare from back in Vietnam when my buddy stepped on a mine and both his legs were blown off.

"I'd get myself so totally wiped out that when I did finally go off and sleep, I wouldn't dream, or if I did, I wouldn't remember it when I woke up."

Shad Meshad, a psychologist and executive director of the Vietnam Veterans Aid Foundation, refers to such men as "action junkies." They spend unbelievably long hours at work, taking on onerous assignments others shy away from, partly to shield themselves from unwanted thoughts and emotions and also to reexperience the sort of thrill they knew during the war. "It sets up a combat situation, just as if they were crawling through the jungles after a sniper," Meshad observes.

But Meshad says it has become more and more difficult for Vietnam veterans in managerial and professional positions to keep themselves together if they have not come to grips with their feelings about the war. Increasing numbers of them have been calling him and other counselors since the late 1980s, he reports, and he predicts many more will surface in the mid-1990s. They face greater stresses at work, for one thing. In the wake of economic recessions, layoffs, and business failures, "there are tremendous pressures on these upper-echelon guys, and additional pressures require additional numbing—more drinking, more smoking, less time with their families," Meshad notes. "You can really see it now that they are in their forties. They look older than other men their age."

WINNING BATTLES BUT LOSING THE WAR

In addition to wearing themselves out, hard-driving Vietnam veteran managers also wear out those with whom they work. They may drive their staffs as hard as they drive themselves, and they can be ornery with their superiors.

"They're not people who blithely follow along behind the person carrying the banner that says, 'I'm the Boss,' " notes Robert E. McFarland, Ph.D., a psychologist at the Veterans Administration Medical Center in North Chicago, Illinois. "They've been in that position before. They did that naively for a while as youngsters in a jungle, and that's a mistake they're not going to repeat."

Where others zealously fall in line behind upper management in hopes of making it into the executive suite, Vietnam veterans "scrutinize the moral environment of the workplace," McFarland says. "They pose some very problematic questions at work. In war they had to lay aside their morality as human beings, and many of them are not willing to do that again."

Back when they were Young Turks in their companies, their uppity behavior may actually have advanced their careers by distinguishing them as self-starters. But by the time they enter middle age, such behavior no longer endears them to their superiors.

"They do well for a number of years, they climb the ladder and look quite good; then, when they reach a mid-management level, it tends to unravel and many times falls apart completely," says McFarland. They either plateau in their careers or lose their jobs or quit.

Chris Walker, a forty-four-year-old vice president at a bank in Cincinnati, is a case in point. He started out as a teller upon his return from the war, took college and graduate courses at night through a program the bank offered employees, and over the next decade and a half gradually ascended up through the ranks to middle management.

Yet for more than five years now, Chris has been passed over for promotions. On several occasions, he has been told he is way too impolitic to make it into the executive ranks. "I won some battles but lost the war," Chris puts it. Whenever he disagreed with a superior, he said so. His behavior antagonized some people, but there was always someone high up in the chain of command who protected him.

"I'd get so angry sometimes in meetings," recalls Chris, "I'd tell a manager to go fuck himself. The vice president who was running the meeting would tell me to cool down, but by the same token, he'd be sitting at the end of the table smiling while I went after the guy."

Chris admits regretting that he will never make it into senior management or earn the kind of money that would allow him to send his three-year-old daughter to private school. But he says the battles he has fought have been noble ones. Generally, his scuffles have been with people above him who enacted policies Chris considered detrimental to his staff.

"There were a couple of times I started to sell out," he indicated, "and I couldn't go home and look at myself in the mirror. They were dangling carrots in front of me—promotions I'd get if I did things they wanted me to do that I knew damn well were bad for my people, and I couldn't do it. I had to fight."

A front-line combat officer during the war, Chris holds to some principles that might be seen as unusual in the corporate world of the 1990s. "What's important," he declared, "is keeping the people under you employed and being your own man.

"I don't believe that the people who run the company have all the goddamn answers. I've been a business manager now for twelve years, and I don't want some guy who has been with the bank maybe a year and doesn't know what's happening at my level sitting up there and telling my team what is important and what isn't."

GUILTY SURVIVORS

According to Robert McFarland, it is survival guilt that prevents veterans like Chris from moving beyond the middle rung of their career ladders. "In their heart of hearts," said McFarland, "they believe they are not supposed to succeed. They believe they are not supposed to drink fully from the cup of life because they carry a terrible burden. They have friends who died, and they believe they could have prevented those people from dying if only they had done something."

In nearly every case, when McFarland probes a veteran's stories of loss and survival, he discovers that it would have been impossible for the vet to have saved his buddies. "Nonetheless," McFarland stated, "these men feel their penalty is to be unhappy, and not being successful is part of being unhappy."

During my conversation with Chris Walker, in the midst of telling me how he helped a woman on his staff find another job after the bank eliminated her position, he suddenly launched into a description of a battle in Vietnam. Two of his buddies took direct hits: one died and the other had his face blown off.

"My buddy was dead, but I was still alive," Chris said in a sad, reflective voice strikingly unlike his confident tone of a moment before. "Three other men around me were also dead, and I wasn't even scratched. I felt like I should have walked away with *something*. It still bothers me. When we started getting hit, I ran for cover. If I'd pulled my buddy with me, maybe he'd be alive today."

Chris quickly returned to the earlier topic he'd been discussing, saying he wasn't sure why that incident in Vietnam had popped into his mind. But the moral of both stories is clear. Chris believes he must atone for having survived when his buddies did not. His atonement consists, on the one hand, of limiting his own personal fulfillment, and on the other, of ensuring he never again lets someone die whom he can rescue. When his co-worker was about to endure a symbolic death by losing her job, Chris rushed to find her other employment.

TOUGH GUYS: THE COMMANDER MENTALITY

Different Vietnam veteran managers respond to corporate up-heavals in different ways, partly depending upon what baggage they still carry from the war.

In World War II the average American soldier was twenty-six years old, but in the Vietnam War he was nineteen. By the time men went off to fight in World War II, they had completed the major tasks of early adulthood. They'd left home, married or become engaged, and entered a career. Soldiers in the Vietnam War, on the other hand, had accomplished little if any of that by the time they were whisked off to the jungle. Their adult iden-tities had not yet been formed. For Vietnam vets, the war was a crucial factor in the development of skills, fears, and predilec-tions that continue to define who they are as adults.

Some men who were officers in Vietnam have retained what might be called a *commander mentality.* In the military they learned to put the goals of the organization above their per-sonal feelings, and they do the same in the corporate setting. Confronted with the necessity of laying off people who work under them, such men take a pragmatic, unsentimental ap-proach. "In combat, I had to send people out knowing some of them would be killed," one of them said to me. "I didn't like it, but I had to do it, and these cutbacks are kind of the same way. I wish the people didn't have to go, but if the company is to sur-vive and be strong, they do, and it's my job to carry that out."

Such veterans typically deny that Vietnam had any serious or lasting effect on them. They take pride in the fact that they have led stable, successful adult lives, free of remorse and all the symptoms of PTSD, ever since they got out of the service.

But according to David Grady, a therapist at Friends Hospital in Philadelphia, these men have not left their war experiences behind. They merely re-create in their civilian lives the role they played in Vietnam. At home, they bark orders at their wives and children, and for their livelihood they work at firms where the corporate culture is paramilitary—where the chain of command is strictly hierarchical and predominately male, and managers are given clear objectives.

Within such an environment, a veteran with a commander mentality is highly valued by upper management because he lets nothing get in the way of the successful completion of projects assigned him. "Everything and everyone gets subordinated to the mission," Grady explained.

But when they reach the critical junction of midlife and mid-career, these men may find the next step up the corporate ladder beyond their reach. At a certain point, their single-minded devotion to getting the job done no longer furthers their careers.

As Grady explained, "At the higher levels of management, the political dimension becomes more important. But guys who were successful in a command role in the war remain very mission-oriented. They don't pay enough attention to who likes them or who they need to support or oppose."

Rather than ditch their commander mentality once it becomes obsolete, they retreat further into it, pushing themselves and their staffs ever harder to beat deadlines and show their worth. "They attempt to deal with the problem the same way someone would in combat," Grady analogized. "If you're a commander in combat and you run up against a hurdle, you try to overpower it. But that's not really what's called for in this case, and they get bypassed by guys who are more political."

When their bosses are suddenly their junior by years or they are demoted after a corporate reorganization, these men suffer a crisis. For the first time in their lives, they feel vulnerable, in-adequate, and painfully alone. Unwilling to appear weak in front of co-workers or spouses, they put forward a false macho front to those who could provide them with empathy and support.

Some do eventually seek counseling, but Grady and other therapists tell me they seldom have much interest in gaining insight about themselves. Typically they just want reassurance that they are okay. Once they convince themselves they are just going through a "normal midlife crisis" or "career burnout," they quit treatment.

Few men with a commander mentality permit themselves to experience a full-fledged crash or confront the awkward personal questions that a crash provokes. After the initial shock, they pull themselves back together and return to the plateau they have reached within their companies.

Such men may be setting themselves up for bigger troubles in the future, however. "They have made it to middle age without the basic tools necessary for the later stages of life," Grady noted. "They haven't come to grips with the way their lives have gone so far, and they haven't made a conscious decision about whether they want to continue living that way in the future."

PIECING TOGETHER A SELF

Caldwell ("Cal") Wilson, forty-two, is one man who did come to grips with his past and chart a new course for himself. A few years ago he stopped torturing himself the way he had done ever since the war, and he switched into an occupation that suits him better than any he had pursued in the past.

As manager of equipment purchases and repairs for a motion picture production company in Los Angeles, he does work that calls upon his best talents and integrates several longstanding interests. He works with machinery, a love that goes back to his boyhood; he's called upon to make quick decisions under pressure, an ability he mastered as a nineteen-year-old infantryman in Vietnam; he applies the technical skills he acquired as an engineering major in college; and because most of the filming is done on location, he spends much of his time outdoors, something he enjoyed in his previous job.

Cal had held his previous job as a land surveyor for a county in northern California for a dozen years, from the time he graduated college until his late thirties. It made poor use of his training and aptitudes and frequently left him bored. He had taken the job and stayed with it so long, he explained, for the solitude it afforded.

"It goes back to when I came out of Vietnam. I was really fucked up," said Cal, a bearded man with deep lines in his face from too many hours in the sun and too many internal struggles. "I didn't associate with people hardly at all for a long while after I came back. There were days I didn't say more than ten words to anybody.

"I didn't trust people and I didn't trust myself. For a number of years, I carried a gun in my boot, and a couple of times I almost fired it."

After Cal took some shrapnel in his gut during his tenth month in Vietnam, he was shipped home, and a half year later, having recovered from his injury, he enrolled for the fall 1969 semester at Chico State College. From the start he had trouble relating to other students there. On the one side were the men in the special dormitory where Cal had been assigned—other Vietnam veterans who continually retold war stories Cal found repugnant. On the other side were the antiwar protesters, with whose politics Cal basically agreed.

But then a couple of the leaders of the local SDS chapter stopped him en route to class one day and invited him to join their organization. "They talked about all the girls I could screw if I joined their movement and the fantastic dope I would get," Cal remembers. "They were no different from the grunts back in Vietnam, except they had long hair."

So Cal kept to himself during college, and upon graduation, he took the job as land surveyor for a county nearby and continued his self-imposed isolation. With hindsight, he recognizes that the job represented as well "a chance to do something positive outdoors, something constructive."

Not until recently did Cal begin to come out of his shell and make friends. During his years as a surveyor, he informed me, only two people broke through the wall he constructed around himself. The first was a woman who lived in his apartment building. "Becky had grown up in Los Angeles and run around with some pretty dangerous guys before she met me. I guess she could tell I wasn't crazy," said Cal of this woman, a commercial artist with whom he recently celebrated his fifteenth wedding anniversary. "I don't know what she saw in me at first. I think I was kind of like a Good Samaritan project for her when she met me."

Cal says he doubts he would be alive today if it weren't for Becky. Early in their relationship, she made him promise never to commit suicide, a vow he considered odd at the time. But a few years ago he discovered just how prescient she had been. The one other person with whom Cal had gotten close, a man he worked with in the surveyor's office, died in an automobile accident, and his death tore Cal apart.

Following the funeral, Cal sank into a deep depression and quit his job. "I couldn't stand doing anything," he recalls. "You would have thought that being in Vietnam, seeing people blown up, would have prepared me to deal with death, but it didn't. If I hadn't made that no-suicide promise to Becky, I would definitely have done myself in."

Instead, what Cal did was to load his Toyota with camping equipment and food and head for the Sierra Nevada. Up in the mountains he grieved for his friend and for the dozens of men he'd known in Vietnam who had died.

THE RITUAL OF LETTING GO

For five weeks, Becky didn't see Cal. He drove into town a couple of times to call her, but otherwise he remained alone with his own thoughts and emotions.

The first few days after he set up camp, Cal did little except cry, and the next several he mostly slept—peacefully at first, until the nightmares began. "Sometimes they got so bad," he said, "I'd wake up in the morning and the sleeping bag would be soaking wet with sweat."

Directly and defenselessly, Cal faced the horrors he had suppressed for close to two decades. The nightmares gave way to flashbacks and fits of rage, and then, at some point during his third week in the wilderness, he started engaging in what he describes as "weird nature rites." With his bare hands, Cal would dig a deep hole in a clearing near his campsite and scour the woods nearby for dead animals and seeds he would place in the hole, which he then refilled with dirt. At night he would build fires, into which he sometimes tossed letters he wrote to his father.

Unknowingly, Cal administered to himself a variation of a form of therapy called the Sweat Lodge, which has been successfully used many times with Vietnam veterans since it was first tried in the early 1980s. This approach, based upon Native American healing practices, involves therapists taking a group of veterans into the woods, where for a week they engage in group discussions and ritualistic cleansing ceremonies.

Through the rituals he devised, Cal was "letting go of pain

and symbolically transmuting it to Mother Earth," as a group of psychologists who have studied the Sweat Lodge approach wrote in a paper.

Four years after his return from the mountains, Cal said he was well aware of the purpose of his "weird nature rites." The burial of seeds and dead animals substituted, he suggested, for the funerals he had missed for men who died in Vietnam and the forests Americans destroyed there. As for the ceremony of burning letters to his father, Cal said this was the first time he had confronted his tangled emotions toward his dad.

When Cal was flown home from the hospital in Japan, neither his father nor his mother came to the airport to pick him up. Instead they sent his sister, who explained that their parents couldn't face seeing him. A week or so later, his mother apologized, but his father kept his distance, and when Cal finally tried to talk with him, some months later, he launched into a diatribe about how Vietnam was different from the war in which he fought. World War II was a noble war, he declared, the Vietnam War was depraved. " 'I've seen the pictures on TV, the women and babies you killed,' " Cal quoted his father saying. "He didn't mean *I* had killed women and children, but that's sure how it sounded. I couldn't deal with it. I left the room and promised myself I would never mention the war around him again."

Cal broke off with his father completely. For nearly twenty years, he scarcely talked to him, and within himself, Cal severed everything he associated with his father. Some of his favorite memories from childhood were of the Saturday mornings he and his dad worked together on electrical gadgets in the basement. So Cal resisted any urge to seek out jobs that would make use of his talents with circuitry.

Much of the content of those letters he wrote to his father up in the mountains related to happy times they'd spent together years ago. Writing and burning them freed him at last, Cal said, to return home and seek out a new career that made use of talents he had developed in his youth and the education he had gotten in college.

Following several long discussions after Cal returned from the mountains, he and Becky decided to make a major change. For years they had talked of moving south to Los Angeles where Becky would have better job opportunities, and now they figured out they could apply the profits from their house toward rent in L.A. until they got established and could buy another home.

Once they got there, a career counselor Cal consulted helped him identify and land the job with the production company, where at first he worked as an assistant before taking over his boss's job when that man left the company.

FACING VIETNAM

In Cal's discussions of his new career during our interview, Vietnam came up several times: not because I pushed the topic or from any preoccupation on Cal's part, but as a point of comparison, much the same way many women I interviewed, in the middle of discussions about their jobs, made reference to experiences they'd had raising their children.

On days when some of his staff are out sick and all the equipment seems to be breaking down, Cal said, "I go into combat mode. The adrenaline starts pumping and I'm in overdrive. As soon as I tackle one trouble spot, I'm on top of the next one."

Cal said he adapted quickly to that feeling of being under fire and even looks forward to it. His new job has sometimes rekindled other emotions from the war, however, which have left Cal more shaken.

For several months, he avoided contact with a Vietnamese

woman the company had hired. "When our eyes met, she instantly knew that I was a vet and I knew she had escaped the country," he recounted. "My guilt was overwhelming. Every time I saw her I got all anxious and depressed. The memories would come back from one time in Vietnam when we shot an old woman we thought was booby-trapped because she had a big box in her hand. Who knows, that woman could have been her grandmother."

Eventually, the Vietnamese woman broke the ice. She came by Cal's office one afternoon and said she wanted to talk. "We ended up talking almost two hours," he recollected. "Her entire family had been killed, and she'd gotten out on the last day of the evacuation. Her stories were horrible, just horrible. She was only twelve years old when she lost both her parents.

"I wanted to say to her, 'I was part of that, I was part of the cause of those atrocities.' But she said, 'No. It's not your fault. You shouldn't feel guilty.' She said she didn't hold anything against the veterans, it was our government that was wrong."

Cal hugged the woman and thanked her before they each went back to work. Apart from his wife, Becky, she was the only person he had hugged since he returned from the war.

part three

Staging

a

Revival

part
three

CHAPTER 8

NAKED CAREER
COUNSELING

Baby boomers who lose or leave their jobs often find themselves unwelcome around town. Former colleagues treat them as though they have a contagious disease. Potential employers, inundated with résumés, are reluctant to grant them an interview. Even friends and family, perceiving them as unstable, shun them.

Only one group of people embraces the career displaced with open arms: the hundreds of thousands of résumé writers, vocational testing specialists, career counselors, and outplacement consultants who earn their living advising the unemployed and unhappily employed. Nothing warms their hearts more than the arrival at their offices of bright but confused baby boomers. Perennially hungry for self-knowledge and possessed of severance funds or savings accounts to pay for advice, baby boomer achievers make ideal clients.

Within the vocational advice industry, competition is intense these days. Membership in the National Career Development Association, a professional organization of career counselors,

grew by 20 percent between 1985 and 1991. The number of listings in the yellow pages under the headings "vocational guidance," "career counseling," and "résumé services" has tripled or
even quadrupled in many cities since the late 1970s.

In interviewing assorted career advisers over the past four
years and reading the books and journals from which they learn
their trade, I've discovered they fall into two camps—those who
subscribe to a *flat-tire* approach and those who adopt a *fork-in-
the-road* model.

A majority of career advisers embrace the flat-tire approach.
When people come to them for help, they evaluate what's
wrong, patch them up, and send them on their way. Some of
these advisers do nothing more than tinker with résumés or tell
their clients what to say at job interviews. Others go a bit farther
and administer vocational tests. Based on the results, they steer
people into one type of job rather than another.

But the growing number of career advisers who subscribe to
the fork-in-the-road model reject that approach. Our society affords adults appallingly few opportunities to pause and reconsider where they have been and where they are headed, these
career advisers point out. Demoralized by pink slips or miserable in jobs that have proven detrimental to their health, people should be encouraged to do some serious soul-searching.
Career advisers who take a fork-in-the-road perspective use
techniques adapted from family therapy, clinical psychology,
and social work to help their clients review decisions made earlier in their lives and choose carefully the criteria they'll use to
make their upcoming career decisions.

When picking a career adviser, it's a case of boomer beware.
If you're not careful, you'll spend a lot of time and money on
simpleminded suggestions that serve only to push you back
onto the same perilous career track you crashed out of.

• • •

TIRE REPAIR SHOPS

Like so many other places in our efficiency-obsessed society, speed is everything in much of the career advice industry. Headhunters, outplacement counselors, résumé writers, and many independent career counselors accept as a guiding tenet of their practice that clients should be placed in jobs as promptly as possible. They put forward a host of humane-sounding reasons. *Job hunting is demoralizing and expensive; why prolong the agony? . . . Almost everybody ends up in the same sort of job they had before anyway. . . . The longer you linger the less marketable you become.*

But if the truth be told, the main motive for hurrying clients along is not the clients' well-being but the career advisers' turnover. Take headhunters, whom American corporations pay $2 billion a year to locate experienced people for specific job openings. A headhunter's business consists of slotting professionals into positions identical or very similar to the ones they currently or recently occupied.

"It costs a headhunter money to let somebody stew in his juices for a while or think about five or six different options," observed Barbara Reinhold, Ed.D., director of Smith College's Career Development Center. "So what a headhunter usually says is, 'You're not marketable in any field except this one.' "

Reinhold pointed out that such a comment can be devastating. "A person who has suffered a career crash can fit their self-esteem on the head of a pin. To have somebody in an official capacity say, 'I'm sorry, you're just not marketable' feels like a death sentence."

Outplacement counselors, brought in by companies at the opposite end of the employment cycle—when they're laying people off—are understandably more upbeat. Their avowed mission is to keep sacked employees optimistic that they will find work.

Yet outplacement counselors, too, advocate swift, narrow job searches. When Dyan Machan, a journalist with *Forbes* magazine, spoke with managers and executives who were victims of downsizing about what they got out of outplacement counseling, she found that they were given "a keen grasp of the obvious." In group lectures and individual sessions, they were told to update their résumés, present themselves well at interviews, and maintain a positive outlook as they look for jobs like the ones they lost. Then they were sent off to big rooms filled with cubicles where they could make phone calls or read newspapers. "Outplacement, at best, is an example of good intentions misplaced," Machan concluded.

The outplacement industry rakes in $600 million a year from corporate directors whose main concern is to keep axed employees busy and sober, lest they bad-mouth the firm and demoralize other workers. Sociologically speaking, the function of outplacement counseling is not to assist the victims of corporate downsizings but to keep them out of the way.

Business Week magazine rightly suggested that the money an employer pays to an outplacement firm might better benefit a laid-off manager if it were added to his or her severance fund. For a typical $60,000-a-year manager, the amount comes to around $10,000, many times what it would cost to hire a career adviser on one's own.

THE REVOLVING DOOR

Career advisers paid by job seekers rather than by their former employers or potential employers might reasonably be expected to take a more client-centered approach. Whether they actually do so, however, depends upon their orientation. Most advisers, regardless of who pays them, neglect to probe very deeply into their clients' needs or desires before sending them back to the work world.

Résumé-writing services are probably the assistance most frequently sought by career crashers. For fees ranging from $50 to $1,000, these establishments will transform how well someone looks on paper. But they, too, pursue a revolving-door policy. "Turnaround time is the critical factor in their business. They make their cash by working fast," Barbara Reinhold has found. She said there's little point asking a résumé writer to help you market yourself for a different kind of job than you have held in the past. "They'll say, 'No, we can't write your résumé that way; you don't have the skills for that, you don't have the experience.'"

Likewise, vocational advisers who go by the official title of "career counselor," although they do more than merely revise résumés, are generally of the flat-tire model. They meet with clients no more than three to ten times each and rely on mechanical methods for assessing people and directing them back onto career tracks.

A main tool of the career counselor's trade is standardized testing. They sit people down with pencil and paper—or if they've gone higher tech, at a computer screen—and have them answer questions from tests that go by names like Career Maturity Inventory Attitude Scale, Sixteen Personality Factor Questionnaire, Values Card Sort, and Strong-Campbell Interest Inventory. Based on the results of the tests, career counselors make recommendations about where clients should hunt for jobs.

Creatively applied, aptitude and interest tests can help people think more openly about what they want to do with their lives. But career counselors too often use the tests in precisely the reverse way—to *exclude* possibilities. Armed with the results of a set of tests, career counselors shoot holes in clients' dreams.

In the public mind, vocational tests carry the imprimatur of science. In reality, studies show that people who are reasonably bright can assess their own abilities and preferences as well or better than do the tests. The appeal of the tests is not so different, in fact, from what draws people to astrology. Sophisticated testers, like sophisticated astrologers, basically feed back in more elaborate lingo the information they're given by the client. They validate and explicate what people suspect about themselves.

Some of the reports that come back from vocational tests even sound like astrological readings. "Your answers to the Myers-Briggs Type Indicator questions came out the type called Introverted Thinking with Intuition," begins an actual computer-generated summary from one of the most widely used tests in the career counseling industry. "INTPs are quiet, reserved, detachedly curious, and quite adaptable so long as their ruling principles are not violated."

The report goes on to warn: "If feeling values are ignored too much, they may build up pressure and explode in most inappropriate ways."

People who have spent little or no time working, such as teenagers and young adults, for whom vocational exams were devised in the first place, may profit from such sketches. Experienced career advisers tell me, however, that the profiles are of little use to most baby boomers.

Mary Lynne Musgrove goes so far as to proclaim: "I almost never meet a person who's gotten the answers from a test." The results that emerge raise more questions than they settle, according to Musgrove. She offered the hypothetical example of a corporate manager who pinpointed what she likes most and least about her job. With the help of a test, she clarified that she hates office politics and enjoys something she spends only a small percentage of her time doing, namely, the preparation of budgets.

Should this woman, on the basis of insights gleaned from the test, look for a job as budget manager? Musgrove says not. She would want to ask the woman a series of probing questions before encouraging her to move in *any* particular direction. "What is it about working with numbers? Is she really intrigued with numbers, or is this an isolated situation? Does she only like working with budgets because it gets her out of the office politics? What does she do with numbers at home? What does she do when her bank statement comes? Does she throw it in the drawer with the other three years' worth or does she love to sit there and find every penny? Did she ever take any math courses in school? How were they for her? When was the last time she took one? Why didn't she take any more after that?

"Sometimes," Musgrove observed, "it isn't that a person really likes numbers. It's that her work with numbers is the only part of her job that gives her a tangible, measurable outcome."

Musgrove said if she pursues her line of questioning further, she might discover that this woman has long wanted to do something far removed from budgets and finance but never let herself express those desires. Maybe what she actually wants to design is not her division's budget, but the company's advertising. Perhaps when she was young, an influential parent or teacher persuaded this woman to go into something more "practical."

Often in her counseling practice, Musgrove will devote several sessions with a client to an examination of how the person ended up in something other than what she really loves—a topic that career counselors who operate from the flat-tire model would seldom even broach.

FACING THE FORK IN THE ROAD

Musgrove is part of a small, unfederated, but growing breed of career advisers who seek to do more for their clients than administer tests or get them speedily reemployed. These career advisers maintain, in fact, that finding another job is not the most important task a person faces during a career crash.

While anyone's natural inclination after losing or leaving a job is to seek, as swiftly as possible, a replacement position, that impulse may not be a sound one. Better to proceed slowly and critically, these advisers contend, even if that means dipping deeply into savings or taking part-time or temporary work to feed the kids. To rush into another job is often to set oneself up for failure. A rebound job, like a rebound relationship, may prove comforting at first, but turn out to be even worse than the situation left behind.

Advisers who subscribe to the fork-in-the-road model consider it a professional obligation to slow up their baby boomer clients and get them to engage in some serious self-reflection. Rather than apply the same tools of their trade in the same mechanical ways to everyone who walks through their office door, they tailor their approach to the particular needs of individual clients. Having supplemented their training in vocational guidance with courses in marriage counseling, social work, cognitive psychology, or psychotherapy, they have a variety of techniques to choose from. With one client they may use a standard aptitude test, with another a "vocational genogram"—a family tree showing the career choices of the person's siblings, parents, grandparents, aunts, and uncles. With some clients, most of the counseling sessions are spent on job-related matters, while with others the primary focus is on relationships and lifestyle issues.

In deciding how best to assist a crashing client, these advisers pay a lot of attention to how the person got into her career in the first place. Did she prematurely foreclose her options like the men and women in a previous chapter? Or did she bounce from job to job before finally settling into a career track? Each type requires very different sorts of counseling, maintains career adviser Judith Grutter.

For people who prematurely foreclosed their options as kids, orthodox methods of career counseling aren't much use, Grutter told me. If the usual battery of vocational tests is administered, the results will show that they should remain in the profession they originally entered. "You can only respond positively to interests that you've experienced," noted Grutter. "A test doesn't give a picture of what a person hasn't been exposed to that they might be happier doing."

Vocational testing may encourage people who prematurely foreclosed to do exactly what they should not—jump right back into their current field or switch to a related one. "Their inclination is to make another quick decision," Grutter said. "The foreclosed person wants closure again but requires the opposite if they're going to be satisfied later in life. They need to open up."

Using techniques derived from Gestalt psychology, Grutter pushes her foreclosed clients to get back in touch with the activities that attracted them in their youth. She may spend entire counseling sessions talking with them about what they were like at age six or seven or ask them to go back and play games they used to enjoy. "They shut down their exploration process very early in life, usually by seventh or eighth grade. I try to tap in to who they were before they shut down," she said, "and not let them commit again to a career before they explore some of those earlier parts of themselves."

She draws a sharp contrast between prematurely foreclosed baby boomers and the second group, who throughout their teens and even early twenties bummed around in assorted college courses and full-time or part-time jobs before committing to a particular vocation. These boomers, when they lose or leave their jobs, go through what Grutter calls "a second moratorium." In the process of rejecting their current profession as too stressful, immoral, or dull, they idealize any other line of work that sounds like more fun.

Grutter presses such clients to think very concretely about what they want the next portion of their lives to be like. Romantic fantasies won't do. If someone says he is ready to give up his six-figure income and live more simply, she asks him to pinpoint exactly what he's willing to forgo: Expensive evenings out? Life insurance? A child's college education?

Grutter also insists that her clients look closely at whatever new jobs they are considering. A corporate manager who says she wants to become a schoolteacher in order to rescue disadvantaged children might be asked, for example, to go out and interview four or five teachers about what they do all day. Confronted with the reality that most of a teacher's time is spent preparing classes, grading papers, and punishing misbehavior, she might rethink her options. Instead of going back to college to become a classroom teacher, she may decide to keep her current job but reduce her hours and tutor in the evenings. Even if she decides to make a major career change, Grutter might route her toward a vocation within the education field—as an educational administrator, say, or a school psychologist—something that will give her more of the power and professional status to which she is accustomed.

To illustrate how much patience may be required to make a mature career change, Grutter tells the story of a woman she counseled for three years. At the beginning of that time, she was making $200,000 a year as an unhappy thirty-seven-year-old dermatologist in Los Angeles. By the end, she had a farm in northern California where she grew organic vegetables and with luck would earn a quarter of her old income.

Early on, all she knew was that she hated her job and wanted to do something socially responsible. After a number of counseling sessions, she was able to specify that she wanted to get out of L.A., go into an agricultural field of some sort, and have her own business.

Rather than let this woman go cold turkey from her high-rise condo and Mercedes convertible to a remote ranch and a pickup truck, Grutter mapped out a several-step transition process. First the woman resigned from her practice and worked as a consultant with a cosmetics company, a move that gave her the chance to drive around California in search of farm land and at the same time to test out how she really felt about leaving the medical profession and her friends in L.A. During that period of several months, she and Grutter worked together to select from the various agricultural careers open to her one that could provide a sustainable income while allowing her to produce a crop she could be proud of.

Even once she bought her farm, quit medicine entirely, sold her condominium, and moved to the country, at Grutter's advice she kept one foot in her old profession. She consulted part-time for the county health department until her farming business got off the ground and she had tested how well she liked rural life.

FAMILY MATTERS

Career counselors who subscribe to the fork-in-the road model view the selection of an alternative vocation as something far more profound than simply a search for a paycheck. They impress upon their clients that in choosing a new profession, they are also choosing a new place for themselves in the world—not only in the world of work, but in the larger society.

By virtue of their choice of jobs, baby boomers opt for one city over another, one circle of acquaintances over another, one economic stratum over another. They also select the positions they will occupy within their households in the future. Depending upon which jobs they go after, they become more involved as parents or less so or take on the role of chief bread-winner or give it up.

Baby boomers reposition themselves within another family

context as well when they change jobs, one which several career counselors say is the most important of all: *They alter their relationships within their family of origin.* By electing one career course over another, they draw closer to or move farther away from their parents and siblings.

Sometimes the realignment is obvious. When prematurely foreclosed men and women ditch the professions they entered at their parents' behest, they declare themselves independent of their parents. And vice versa, when rebels give up their countercultural jobs for conventional ones, they symbolically reunite with their parents. Frequently, though, the realignments are more subtle.

In a study of people who changed professions, Hanna Chusid and Larry Cochran of the University of British Columbia describe an architect named Alice, who at age thirty-six became a stockbroker. In so doing, she stopped playing the dutiful daughter, a role she'd assumed in family and work settings since childhood. As an architect, Alice had constantly found herself trying to satisfy people she described as "nonsupporters" and "takers," terms she also applied to her mother. By switching from architecture to securities, Alice moved away—literally and symbolically—from her mother and toward her sister and her aunt, who were less overbearing and more supportive. She stopped speaking to her mother and began seeing her sister more frequently. And in her new profession, her colleagues tended to resemble her aunt and her sister, Chusid and Cochran report.

Other career changers whom Chusid and Cochran studied drew rewardingly *closer* to their mothers or fathers instead of splitting off from them. One man had rebelled against his father's wishes by becoming a theater director. Upon leaving that profession to become a businessman, he began talking with his father far more frequently.

Of course, the adjustments in parent-child relationships following career changes are not invariably so healthy. One reason some career advisers have begun paying more attention to family matters is a growing awareness that people at midlife may try to mend relationships by changing vocations, only to end up worse off for the effort.

One psychoanalyst, Roberta Satow, Ph.D., told me about a woman she was counseling who had become seriously depressed after a failed career change. "She had hoped," said Satow, "that by leaving her first career she was going to leave her mother behind. She felt that her first career as a schoolteacher reflected her mother's values, and in moving away from that career she moved away from her mother's value system toward her father's value system. She chose a field with very few women, a field that involves a lot of mechanical aptitude, which she identifies with her father."

By way of her career switch, Satow's client effected a long-desired link to her father. The two of them had much more to talk about and spent more time together. She also stopped pretending to be the nurturing altruist her mother had raised her to be and followed up on interests she'd ignored since childhood.

But those positive dimensions of her decision were only half the story. Her choice of a second profession, far from resolving her troubled relationship with her mother, actually reproduced it. "She selected a career where you have to be very, very careful to do the work just right, which is a replication of her relationship with her mother. Her mother is very critical; everything has to be exactly perfect. So on the one hand she was consciously moving away from her mother, but on the other, she was unconsciously moving even closer to her."

Satow said her client changed careers before she had enough understanding of the real meaning of what she was doing. Through counseling she was being helped to look more deeply into her career choices and identify other, psychologically healthier, options.

JOYCE'S RESOLUTION

Fork-in-the-road career advisers pose quite different questions to their clients than do traditional career counselors. Instead of asking what someone is most qualified to do, they ask about the hidden ramifications of pursuing one career direction over another.

Is the person rushing into a job that will leave her neither happier nor more settled than the one she left? Is she moving farther from her true needs and talents? Is she perpetuating old conflicts with her family by way of her job choice?

If answering such questions sounds like an impossible luxury for people whose self-esteem is sinking while their bills are mounting, several career advisers I interviewed say otherwise. They point to clients of theirs who have done it—people like Joyce Mayfield of Washington, D.C. The career adviser who sent me to Joyce described her as someone who turned the misfortune of losing her job into an opportunity to reconsider who she is and to reunite with members of her family.

The congressman for whom Joyce had worked as an executive assistant for four years had been defeated at the polls. Another politician had offered her a full-time job, but Joyce was pretty certain she would turn him down. Following a series of conversations with her career counselor, she'd decided instead to pursue the far riskier option of starting her own business as an affirmative action consultant to industry and government.

Throughout the election campaign, she had been terrified, she told me, that her boss would lose and she'd have to scrounge up another way to support herself and her eight-year-old daughter. "But after the election, I was relieved," said Joyce, a forty-one-year-old black woman. "I needed autonomy. This was the first job I'd had in a long while where I answered to somebody so totally and had my time so regulated. Now I'm very much into being able to function on my own."

On the one hand, Joyce's choice of a new career is purely logical and practical. In her job she had learned a lot about discrimination statutes and affirmation action programs. The congressman for whom she worked had been a leading opponent in the House of Representatives against the Bush administration's efforts to weaken civil rights legislation. Then too, Joyce had recently completed an MBA program at night and wanted to put her degree to good use.

But there's a more personal side to the story of Joyce's new career choice. Asked to explain why autonomy was so important to her, she replied, "I get that from my father. He never liked working for someone else and only did it when he had no other choice."

Joyce described how she and her father had talked for hours on end when she had moved back home to rural Alabama several years earlier to help care for him in the final months of his battle with cancer. During their conversations, Joyce learned how much her father had valued the one-man business he ran most of his adult life delivering wood and ice to families whose homes lacked electricity.

Hearing him up before dawn chopping wood, and seeing him totally bushed when he returned home at dusk, Joyce had assumed as a child that her father would have preferred to work at the paper mill like the fathers of most of the kids in her school. But no, he told her, he had worked at the mill a couple of times when the family needed more money, and he hated it. At the mill he was but a hired hand, he explained to his daughter; in his delivery business he chose his own hours and provided a service to black people who needed it.

Joyce said she felt the same way about her own current decision. She could assist another white congressman, or she could build a business of her own that would create and protect jobs for blacks.

Her relationship with her mother played a role, too, in her career decision. "I was the one she considered slow," said Joyce, anger and disappointment mingled in her voice. "When I went to school I was always told, 'Your sisters and brother did this or that faster.' One year my mother went to the teacher and asked her to hold me back a year because she thought I hadn't accomplished enough."

The teacher disagreed and passed Joyce on with high grades, but Joyce continued to struggle to win her mother's respect. "My mother wanted one of her children to be a nurse, because she never got to be a nurse herself," she relayed. "So I became a nurse. I finished third in my nursing school class, and I still felt it wasn't enough to prove to her I wasn't the slow one, so I went on and got my B.S. degree.

"I didn't go to the graduation ceremony, though. I had them mail my diploma to my mother. I told her it was hers."

Joyce's more recent receipt of her M.B.A. degree, along with the impending loss of her job, finally broke her out of that impossible contest with her mother and siblings. When Joyce and I spoke, she was in the process of changing the terms of her relationship with her family in an ingenious manner by initiating a family project.

Joyce's plan was to write a grant proposal to a national foundation for public broadcasting to get funds to make a television documentary about one family's firsthand experiences with affirmative action. Joyce, her two sisters, and her brother have all benefited from affirmative action programs, but they hold very different views about these programs. They also live in separate regions of the country and work in quite distinct fields. "We're the Louds of affirmative action," Joyce said, referring to the Loud family, which was the subject of a Public Broadcasting documentary twenty years ago.

At a reunion two weeks before our interview, organized by Joyce at her career adviser's suggestion, the siblings all got together for the first time since their mother's funeral five years before. During a late-night rap session, after spouses and children had gone to bed, Joyce learned something important. "*Everybody* had a tough time with our mother. My relationship with her wasn't as negative as my brother's and one of my sisters'—she was stern and stiff with all of us."

That knowledge, along with the bridge Joyce is building to her siblings, has allowed her to appreciate a valuable inheritance she received from her mother, a personality trait she needs as an aspiring entrepreneur. "My mother was strong and willful. She gave me the ability to persevere no matter what," Joyce said proudly.

Joyce's story is the sort that gives career crashes a good name. For the person who confronts a crash squarely, losing or leaving a job can be an occasion for pulling one's life together, for resolving old conflicts and forging new ties, for retracing one's steps to recover talents and ambitions inadvertently left behind.

BACK TO SCHOOL

Asked in a national survey what they would do if they won the lottery, one in five adult Americans said they would return to school. Amazingly, that option was as popular as quitting one's job and not working at all.

For baby boomer professionals, many of whom enjoyed college the first time around, campuses can be particularly alluring places to turn to find a new life at midlife. And few boomers wait to win the lottery to go back; on the contrary, they often make the move when they're down on their luck. Reports Joan Levine, Ph.D., a therapist in New York City: "Any key experience can activate a person, but usually it's something negative—you become very sick, you get fired, you grow so miserable in your profession that you feel like a victim of your first career choice. Anything that is an assault on who you think you are can motivate you to go back."

For her doctoral dissertation in clinical psychology, Levine conducted an intensive study of sixteen men and women, aged thirty to forty-five, who left their first professions and enrolled in graduate school. She completed that research in 1986, and since then, she's developed a reputation as an expert in counseling people through the difficult period of transition out of a career and into the student role.

Her familiarity with the situations of many dozens of baby boomers who have gone back to school has made Levine eager to dispel a misconception she says is widely held both by the public and by mental health professionals. "There's this notion that people who go back to school are unstable characters," she says, "people who can't commit to a marriage, who can't commit to a career, who basically can't commit to anything."

On the contrary, Levine has found back-to-schoolers devoted in their marriages and other relationships and deeply committed to their first careers before they crashed out of them. They do not take lightly their decisions to leave those careers to return to campus. In opting to become students again, they commit themselves to drastic reductions in income and status for anywhere from two to ten years, and long hours alone in libraries.

Although some psychoanalysts may suspect returning students of running away from internal or interpersonal problems, those Levine has met were generally in the process of *resolving* their conflicts. "They felt frustrated in their work and wanted to see if they could turn it around, and in most cases the outcome was positive. They were much happier in their second career than in their first. They achieved what they had set out to achieve."

Rather than running away from themselves, they asserted who they really were. One man, a physician who gave up his practice and entered art school, told Levine he felt he had come out of the closet.

Baby boomers who return to campus tend to be highly pleased with their decision. The back-to-schoolers I met made statements like, "I have never been happier" and "I hear a voice that says, 'This is what you were born to do.'"

NANCY'S LONG WAY BACK

If everyone agreed they had done the right thing in returning to campus, they differed greatly in how they got there. Some applied to graduate school almost immediately when their first career went awry. One man, a forty-year-old purchasing specialist for a computer firm, went directly from a meeting in which his boss laid him off to a university a few blocks away, where he filled out an application form for admission to the school of education. "The newspapers were full of stories about a teacher shortage," he said. "I'd had a notion to go into teaching ever since my daughter, who was in high school, had entered first grade. I figured, it's now or never." More commonly, though, baby boomers take months or even years to pull themselves away from their first careers and into a graduate program.

Between the time Nancy Marshall first considered enrolling as a graduate student in comparative literature and the day she actually did so, almost ten years passed. A forty-three-year-old former lawyer currently in her second year of a doctoral program at the University of Chicago, she depicts her return to student status as the natural culmination of a lengthy journey—one that began in her youth and took a gigantic detour after college.

During our conversation, which took place in the tiny, book-filled office she shares with another student, Nancy told a story identical in outline to the stories I heard from several other baby boomer professionals who went back to school. She had been seriously interested in literature since childhood, but not until midlife did she find the nerve to try to make a living in such an "impractical" field.

Nancy's passion for literature developed in second grade. The only child of closely knit parents, she remembers feeling lonely in her early years, until she learned to read and could retreat into her room and immerse herself in fictional worlds. Throughout secondary school, her favorite classes were English and French, and during her first two years at Wellesley College she majored in both.

It was during her junior year that she got swept off track. "In 1969, it just seemed wrong to go off and be a literature professor in some sort of ivy-covered tower," Nancy recalled. "Seeing everybody getting locked up in jail in the antiwar protests, I felt I had to help in some way, and I decided to become a criminal defense lawyer."

Nancy switched her major to political science, joined a campus antiwar group, and two years later went off to Stanford Law School, where she volunteered her time to attorneys defending radicals. It was thrilling work, she said, as were her early years as a Legal Aid lawyer in San Francisco after she got her J.D. degree.

But somewhere in the late 1970s, around Nancy's thirtieth birthday, she began to find herself short of energy at the office, unable to bring much enthusiasm to the briefs she was writing. She still cared about the people she defended (the New Left having dissipated by then, most Legal Aid clients were poor folks), but the work itself failed to hold her interest. "The actual practice of law seemed very mechanical and boring to me," she said. "I dreaded writing briefs and waiting for hours on end in court for a case to be called."

Nancy's first, tentative step out of the legal profession came in 1979, when she took a course in French literature at San Francisco State University one evening a week. Although she'd signed up for the class mostly for fun, she did so well that the professor urged her to apply for full-time graduate study.

The idea of returning to school instantly appealed to her, but she didn't treat it seriously, Nancy said. Like many people, she had trouble granting herself permission to throw away all the professional training, expertise, and status she had gained in her first career. "Just because I was burned out in my job, did that give me the right to behave like an overgrown adolescent?" she asked herself.

So Nancy left the Legal Aid office and took a job teaching criminal law at the University of San Francisco. She assumed—correctly—that contact with bright, enthusiastic students would revitalize her and that the students would appreciate the politically informed perspective she brought to her lectures.

What she had not anticipated were the other obligations that come with being a law school professor. In addition to teaching, she was expected to conduct research and prepare scholarly articles. But whenever she sat down to write, she experienced writer's block. "It was very particular," she recollected. "I couldn't come up with an article that would satisfy a law faculty, but in the course I was taking at night on British poetry, I wrote A-plus papers.

"What I wanted to write about was Milton and metaphor, not the law. I came to feel false. I wasn't doing part of the job they were paying me to do, and I wasn't doing what I myself really wanted to be doing, either."

Inauthenticity is the mother of reinvention. When you no longer feel legitimate, you change your perspective on things. Nancy, having tried and failed to find within her profession a way to put her values and talents to good use, opened herself to new ways of thinking. Ivy-covered towers stopped looking so remote or irrelevant to her.

"I took a graduate seminar at Berkeley in eighty-eight," she said, "on the trendy French theorists—Foucault, Kristeva, Derrida—and the discussions were very political. There was real excitement in the air. They were overthrowing the literary canon of the past three hundred years and bringing women and people of color into the curriculum.

"In that three-month class, we talked more about strategies for social change than I had in the whole past fifteen years at the Legal Aid office or the law school."

No longer did she merely desire a new life. She felt morally justified in entering it.

WHAT WOULD THE FAMILY SAY?

To outsiders, a person's return to college may appear to be a regressive act, an attempt to recapture lost youth. But according to those who have actually gone back, nothing could be further from the truth. They are quite articulate about how their decision to train for a new profession resolved old conflicts and allowed them to move forward.

For Nancy Marshall, the conflict she was able to put to rest was ultimately over self-worth. Asked on graduate school application forms why she had chosen to apply, Nancy responded: "At age forty, I finally have the courage to wrestle with Flaubert and Virginia Woolf. So comforting had literature been in my formative years, as a college student I wasn't up to criticizing the great masters or tearing their works apart." Law had seemed not only more politically acceptable back then, Nancy honestly informed the graduate school admissions committees; it also felt safer.

For other baby boomers, the conflict that needs to be sorted out before returning to school is of a different order entirely, particularly if they are married and have children. What right, they wonder, do they have to deprive their families of income and attention?

"They feel terribly out of sync with their spouses," Joan Levine said of several people she studied in the course of her research. "Here they are making a huge investment of money and energy right at a time when their spouses are beginning to enjoy the fruits of earlier labors and are ready to relax and have some fun."

The simplest way of putting an end to this conflict is to forget about going back to school rather than ruffle the relationship. The second alternative, taken by several people Levine studied, is just the reverse: forget about your family's feelings and go right ahead and enroll in a graduate program.

The likely consequence is a series of battles at home. "You feel guilty, and your guilt feels like another burden on top of all those you're shouldering by being in school," Levine described. "So when you come home from campus and your spouse, who is carrying extra household burdens or taking a second job so you can study, says, 'I had a horrible day, I'm really angry with you,' you snap back. Instead of being understanding and grateful, you feel overburdened by guilt and get defensive and nasty."

A third possibility is to negotiate with your partner. Some couples sat down—in certain cases with the children present—and made agreements about how responsibilities and sacrifices would be divided up over the next several years. At the same time, the ones returning to school tried to allay their family's fears that they would abandon them. They also promised to make an extra effort around the house whenever they could—during school holidays, for example. One man pledged to relocate anywhere in the United States or Europe his wife chose after he completed his degree.

Some people delayed returning to school not because of conflicts within their immediate families but because of lingering issues within their *first* families, the families they were born into. Having chosen their professions partly in the hope that their work might help them resolve conflicts with their parents, they had trouble giving up that work until their goal was achieved.

Meg O'Donnell, who at age thirty-four had just graduated from law school, told me she had come to realize that she majored in psychology in college and went on for a degree in family counseling "because I wanted to understand the dysfunctional family I grew up in." Until she achieved that, she couldn't change careers, she said, even though within a few years of graduating from a school of social work she knew for sure that her profession was not intellectually challenging enough for her.

Depressed as she neared her thirtieth birthday, she consulted a therapist who helped her face the fact that no matter how proficient she became at helping other troubled families, her anguish and resentment toward her alcoholic father and depressed mother would not disappear. On the therapist's advice, she set up meetings with her parents, neither of whom she'd seen in close to ten years, and put her best clinical skills to use.

"I diagnosed them the way I would any disturbed client who came to the clinic where I worked. My diagnosis of my father was paranoid character disorder, and for my mother, bipolar depressive disorder," said Meg. "No two people so seriously disturbed could be expected to parent a child, and knowing that helped a lot. It filled me with pity for them, and for myself as a child living with them, and also with thankfulness that I survived, that I had a good marriage and a lot of talents and ambitions."

Within a few weeks of those meetings, she signed up for the Law School Admissions Test. She scored in the top 10 percent.

KEEP YOUR DAY JOB

By the time Meg investigated law schools, applied to several, got accepted, and enrolled in one, almost a full year had passed. She had plenty of time to disengage from her clients and colleagues at the clinic. So when she mentioned during our discussion that she stayed in her job on a half-time basis throughout law school—in spite of a full load of courses—I was a bit perplexed. After all, her husband, a ranking official at the U.S. Department of Education, was happy to foot the bills, as

Meg had done for him earlier while he completed his master's degree in public administration.

Nor was Meg smugly self-confident she could breeze through law school with half her attention turned elsewhere—an accusation one of her professors made after she skipped his class to attend to a client who had threatened suicide. On the contrary: "I felt dumb in law school," Meg reported. "I found the courses incredibly difficult, and I was embarrassed when professors would ask me questions I couldn't answer. It felt like being in first grade again."

No, Meg kept her counseling job to protect her self-esteem. "At work I felt accomplished, respected; at school I mostly felt inadequate," she explained.

One of the chief complaints returning students have about graduate and professional programs is that they're set up in ways that virtually guarantee students will not be treated like full-fledged adults—regardless of whether they are twenty-two years old or twice that age. Like children in a large family, graduate students vie with one another for the attention of a select group of professors willing to guide them through the maze of courses, examinations, and thesis hearings or with sufficient clout to help them land a good job when they graduate.

Those students who need money (as most do) compete also for the limited number of paid positions available in their programs—jobs that bear a shocking resemblance to baby-sitting. Overseeing freshmen classes or research laboratories for professors who are off doing other things, graduate students are paid hourly wages on a par with what an experienced nanny makes.

Said Joan Levine: "If you have reached a certain level of maturity and professional competence, it's infantilizing to become a student again." She noted that most people she studied continued in their previous professions while in school. Some chose to remain almost *entirely* in their old lives, showing up on campus only to attend classes and never socializing with their fellow students.

None of the back-to-schoolers in my study maintained that degree of separation from campus life. But nearly all experienced alienation. Even those with prior ties to the field they were entering said they felt out of place at times. "The opening week of school I walked into a party and I thought 'My God, I've gone back in time,' " reported Seth Gordon, a first-year medical student who is married to a physician. "It was a big keg party with loud music and people trying to get drunk, like frat parties I went to when I was eighteen."

Seth, thirty-three, was surprised to discover how little he has in common with his classmates, most of whom are ten years younger than he is. "Their concerns in life are very different from mine. They're concerned about what their parents think, when their parents are going to give them more money, and how often to go back home. They still live very much in the orbit of their families."

Seth talked with me right before Christmas, just after he completed his first-semester exams, and he drew a contrast between his own plans for the upcoming holidays and those of his fellow medical students. "While they're all running home to their moms and dads, I'm volunteering in the operating room at the university hospital," he reported. Hoping to become a surgeon, he welcomed the chance to witness some operations early in his medical school career, well before he otherwise would.

Besides, Seth said, his wife would be on call half the week between Christmas and New Year, so they couldn't go very far away in any event. And personally, he needed to stay put and rest up. "I pulled an all nighter this week for the first time in many years," said Seth, "and it practically totaled me. Back in college I used to pull three all nighters in a row sometimes when a project was due and have energy left over for a basketball game afterward. I can't do that anymore."

BEING IN THE MINORITY

Seth's classmates view him as something of a curiosity. When they learned that in his previous career he wrote and produced network television shows, they couldn't fathom why he'd chosen to spend eight exhausting years in classes and residency programs. Some students refuse to accept that he truly intends to practice medicine. More than once he has been asked how his scripts are coming along.

"They assume I'm in medical school to do research for a new television series about doctors," Seth relayed. "I find that mildly humorous and a little offensive. Becoming a doctor is my life now."

Baby boomers who return to school consistently report being viewed as peculiar, both by their classmates and by their instructors. The "normal" older student—the type other students and professors *expect* to encounter—is the returning housewife. In novels, films, and magazine articles, most depictions of midlifers on campus are of women whose nests have emptied. For fifteen or twenty years they carpooled their kids, did volunteer or part-time work way below their capabilities, and dreamed of someday finishing their bachelor's degree or going on for a master's in art history. Finally, with their kids grown, they venture timidly forth from their suburbs and enroll.

Boomer back-to-schoolers couldn't be more different. Ambitious and self-assured, they have not only been out in the work world but have been highly successful there. Some are men, and many if not most are single or childless.

Professors and students alike see them as peculiar and rather intimidating and have trouble knowing how to treat them. "The other students treat me like a combination of older sister and mother-protector," said Maria Mendez, forty-one, a second-year MBA student, of other students in her program. "They depend on me to defend them and speak for them. It can get very uncomfortable."

In her finance class one day, the professor made a couple of lewd jokes, and afterward several of the younger women students asked Maria to speak with the man. "You'll put it better, and he'll take it better coming from you," they told her. Maria agreed to voice their concerns, but the professor became defensive, refused to agree he'd done anything wrong, and a few months later recommended against Maria's application for a special fellowship. "It made me angry that my fellow students put me in that position, and upset with myself that I let them," she said.

She is seldom certain *what* stance to take vis-à-vis the faculty, Maria explained. "Do I treat them as peers, or as professors with a capital 'P'?" asked Maria, who was a high school math teacher for fifteen years before she decided she wanted to make some money and applied to business schools. When she first entered the MBA program, she instinctively addressed faculty by their first names and assumed they'd treat her as an equal. But she soon learned that some professors—particularly the youngest, still in their twenties or early thirties, fresh out of school and insecure about status—were made uneasy by her familiarity.

Now at the halfway point in her MBA training, Maria said she would dearly love the close student-mentor relationship some of the other students have with individual professors. Those students get the plum internships and have the chance to work with professors on their research. One professor has even formed a managerial consulting firm with two of his protégés.

"They've got it made," Maria said of these students, and a

host of studies bear her out. Graduate students who have mentors tend to be happier, better settled, and more productive while in school, and they land superior jobs after graduation and move ahead faster in their subsequent careers.

But middle-aged high achievers are not the sort of folks professors most often select as protégés. "Mentoring utilizes the parental impulse," observes Daniel Levinson, the noted Yale psychologist. Professors seek the same rewards from mentoring as from parenting—a "connection with the forces of youthful energy in the world," Levinson called it, and a chance to help shape the next generation. A mentoring relationship with a professional of forty-plus does not exactly fill the bill.

So for guidance and for fellowship, baby boomers end up turning to the same source that blacks, Jews, Hispanics, gays, lesbians, and every other minority group on campus rely upon: each other.

While younger graduate students zealously compete with one another for the best faculty advisers and highest class rankings, back-to-schoolers form mutual support groups. They work on assignments together, share war stories, and generally help one another.

"You naturally make friends with others in the same boat," said Maria Mendez. "I've found lately, when I go into a new class, or even to the study area at the library, the first thing I do is look around to see if I'm the oldest student there. And if I'm not, I try to introduce myself to the others."

Rare is the weekday, Maria added, that she does not eat a meal with an informal group of older students she referred to as the Elders Eating Society. They meet at a restaurant near campus.

Her younger classmates generally cannot afford to dine out that way. "Your typical student straight out of college is living with two or three other people, sharing one bathroom, and taking loans to buy groceries," Maria said. "A big benefit of coming back to school as a grown-up is that you live better."

Many back-to-schoolers bring to campus at least one decent source of cash, be it long-term savings as in Maria's case, a spouse's income, or a well-paid job they still retain. And those who have none of that, who must rely upon fellowships or campus jobs, may live more comfortably than the average student anyway, by virtue of having been around for a while. Some bought homes years ago and have tiny mortgage payments. Others have been living for a decade in rent-controlled apartments that would cost five times as much on the open market.

HUNGRY TO LEARN

Back-to-schoolers have another advantage over their younger classmates as well, one that is less tangible than money but ultimately more consequential.

They really want to be in school.

People in their early twenties, having spent virtually their entire lives in school, view graduate education as a final leg in a long and tiresome journey. Not so the baby boomer who returns after ten or twenty years away, hungry to learn.

Said Seth Gordon, the TV director-turned-medical-student: "I volunteered for this, so I don't feel med school is depriving me or mistreating me the way some of my classmates do. They express a lot of resentment. 'This assignment is too hard.' 'The teacher is asking us to memorize too much.' Frankly, I don't have those reactions. I feel so privileged to have the chance to become a doctor, I accept whatever med school dishes out."

Baby boomers view their admission to graduate school as deliverance from a life they wanted or needed to leave.

"I had outgrown my first career," Seth recounted. "Hollywood is a good place to work so long as you haven't grown up too much. Most TV shows and movies you work on are geared to teenagers, and the Hollywood lifestyle is kind of like a teenage boy's dream come true. Fame, fortune, fancy cars, pretty girls.

"Being a Hollywood insider," he added, continuing the comparison, "is like being on student council in high school. It's a big clique, and you've got to expend a lot of energy to stay in that clique. At a certain point I just didn't want to exert that effort anymore. I was measuring my worth in the world by whose parties I got invited to."

His emotional and physical condition had deteriorated badly, Seth let me know, in the half year before he decided to leave Tinseltown. He'd stopped exercising, and he was using a lot of cocaine and alcohol.

Seldom did Seth wake up without a hangover, and had it not been for a phone call from an old college friend one Sunday morning, he figures he might well have remained in a stupor for years. But she caught him early in the day, before he had his psychological defenses in place. Tearfully he confessed his growing despair and asked her to help him find friends outside the entertainment industry.

Seth's friend set him up on a blind date with a fourth-year medical student who lived in her apartment building. Two months after he started dating her, she took him to her medical school graduation ceremony. "The president of the medical school asked all the people in the audience who were doctors to stand and take the Hippocratic Oath," Seth recalled. "I wanted to stand up, too. They were swearing not to abuse their powers, to take care of the sick, and I sat there and thought, 'I want to do something that meaningful with *my* life.' "

A few months later, at the suggestion of his girlfriend (who later became his wife), Seth took a class at UCLA in emergency medical procedures. "I couldn't believe how much I enjoyed learning medicine," he reported. "It would be accurate to say that the next thing I knew I was a premed student.

"Everybody who knew me thought I'd lost my mind. I was a film major in college. I hadn't taken a single science course. I was going to have to go back for a year or more before I could even begin applying to medical school."

Twenty months later, at the end of his first semester of medical school, Seth remained enthralled. Although he was still several years away from embarking on his new career, he said, "I hadn't *lost* my mind—I had *found* it."

CHAPTER 10

VICTORS

Everyone at the start of a career crash feels like a victim, beaten and robbed by a profession. But many people pick themselves up, dust themselves off, and move on.

How do they do it? What are the crucial tasks after losing or leaving a job? What do people do who come out better off, or at the least, relatively unscathed? Those questions were constantly on my mind as I listened to the diverse stories of baby boomers who contended with the recurrent upheaval of our age.

It's impossible to predict in advance who will survive or flourish after a crash. Neither boomers' backgrounds nor the causes of their crashes foreshadow how they will fare. Among my interviewees, men fared no better than women, Vietnam vets no better than rebels, job leavers no better than job losers.

Those who did bounce back agreed on one fundamental fact: Victory over a career crash is a process that takes place gradually. It begins the moment someone phases out of an old job, and it concludes several weeks, months, or even a year or two later when the person commits to a new one.

The process unfolds in three steps:

> cutting loose
> hanging out
> moving on

The first step is to leave your old job, not just physically but emotionally. The temptation is great to try to hold on to your title and your friendships until you're secure somewhere else. But instead you must let go and put the place behind you.

Only then can you move on to the second stage, where the principal task is to open up your horizons and radically reconsider who you are. Resist the trap of settling into a new work role straightaway. Instead, grant yourself some time to sort through your ambitions and values, unencumbered by a clear professional identity.

When in the third and final stage you do commit to a job, the trick is to do so on different terms than in the past. Rather than relying on your work to give your life meaning and structure, you must abandon the old "Three-S" measure of success (status, salary, and security) in favor of criteria you yourself devise.

These steps—cutting loose, hanging out, and moving on— are actually variations on age-old themes. In 1960, Arnold van Gennep, an anthropologist, described three universal stages in any passage from one status to another. He labeled them "separation," "liminality," and "reincorporation." Whether you're a Zulu child in the process of officially becoming an adult, a young Indian joining Mother Teresa's order of nuns, or a middle-aged American in the midst of a divorce or a career shift, these stages are the ones you must complete to successfully change your status. To put van Gennep's terms in plain English, you must relinquish your old status, go without a clear identity for a while (while you stand on the limen, or threshold), and then adopt a new way of life.

STEP ONE: CUT LOOSE

Whether you loathe your job and voluntarily leave it or love your job and unwillingly lose it, you must put it behind you. Cutting loose involves more than giving up your office and paycheck, it means ceasing to think of yourself as "Susan Turvey, Partner at the law firm of Smith, Jones, and Smith," or "Seth Gordon, big-time Hollywood producer." It also means giving up friendships with most if not all of your former colleagues and ceasing to care about office gossip or how well the company is doing.

Certain aspects of the separation process can be enjoyable, even cathartic. Several baby boomers told me about ceremonies they held, either alone or with others, to celebrate the end of their affiliation with their old employers.

"On the night before my last day at the firm I had a couple of friends bring a bottle of gin to the office after everybody had left," Susan Turvey recounted. "The three of us got crocked while we packed up my stuff."

Recalled Doug Thompson of the evening after he got fired from his position at an insurance company, "I took my company ID card, removed it from the plastic holder, cut it in eight pieces, and burned each of them individually in the kitchen sink."

But another aspect of this first stage is considerably less enjoyable. You have to come to terms with the fact that you have lost something. Even if you quit of your own volition, you give up a set of relationships and an identity that have been important to you.

Many baby boomers, by getting right down to the business of landing a replacement position, deny their loss. They pretend that nothing at their job ever meant a damn to them and they can just move on. Or just as unwisely, they pretend they never left. They make regular visits to their old office or call there every couple of days.

Much as you will never get over the death of a parent or friend if you refuse to own up to the pain of your loss, so, too, you will never get past the loss of your job if you refuse to acknowledge it as a loss. Your emotional business at your old job comes to an end only after you've gone off and mourned its demise.

Those who eventually emerge victorious from career crashes endure a period of profound sadness and seclusion. They differ primarily in when that period occurs. Baby boomers who lose their jobs usually mourn after they depart. Boomers who leave their jobs, on the other hand, often do most of their mourning beforehand. For them it's not the loss of the job that's distressing, but their loss of affection or attachment toward it. The job leaver's grief is more like that of a person who has decided to end a marriage, while the job loser's grief resembles the shock a person feels on learning of a relative's sudden death.

Job leavers and job losers alike tend to be taken by surprise by the amount of grief they experience. "I'm not someone who gets depressed, I'm not someone who sits around feeling sorry for herself, I'm an action-oriented individual," said Paula Dunham of Hartford, Connecticut. "But after I got fired I literally could not leave my bed in the morning. I'd finally get up about eleven o'clock and make a couple of halfhearted job calls, but basically for close to a month I wasn't doing anything except being miserable and getting fat."

The period Paula describes occurred two months after she got downsized out of her managerial job at an insurance company, and actually, she achieved quite a lot. She came to terms with her feelings of having been cruelly betrayed by a company where she'd worked for fifteen years. Certainly Paula accomplished more during her month in mourning than she had her first few weeks out of work, when she ran around Hartford frantically hunting for another job. "I was in a total panic," she recalls. "I burst into offices of people I knew, practically begging them to hire me."

Only after Paula fell to earth and let herself experience the depths of her own fears and regrets could she begin her job search in earnest, in the highly organized and focused way she'd always conducted herself in the past.

Job leavers' crashes, on the other hand, often start with a whimper rather than a bang. Nothing dramatic happens at work to make them see they need to move on. Instead, an overwhelming feeling of grief creeps up on them and they find themselves depressed or in tears without quite knowing why.

"I would return home from work and just sit at the dinner table and cry," said Tracy Collins, who at the time was an associate at a Washington, D.C., law firm. "My husband would ask what was wrong, and all I could tell him was that I was miserable and felt I couldn't continue what I was doing."

For spouses of career crashers, this first stage is indeed a perplexing time. Confused about how to console their seemingly inconsolable mates, they may find themselves baffled as well about the cause of the crash. Except where a person is fired for obvious reasons or quits a detestable job, the cause is typically obscure.

Well liked by the senior partners at her firm, sure to make partner herself, and still keenly interested in the practice of law, Tracy required the help of a therapist to figure out what she was crying over. It took about a dozen sessions before she came to understand that the sorrow she felt was about having prematurely foreclosed her options many years before. The dutiful daughter of a father who was an attorney and a mother who worked as a legal secretary, Tracy had set her sights on a legal career from an early age.

Her third year out of Harvard Law School, when the tears began to flow at dinner, she says was the worst period in her life.

She developed other symptoms as well—insomnia, stomach aches, loss of confidence—all of which she eventually learned in therapy were related to her work.

The agony ceased when she resigned from her firm and began doing free-lance legal writing for a national law journal. Eighteen months later she bills anywhere from ten to twenty hours a week, cares for her year-old daughter, and aptly describes herself, careerwise, as "in limbo."

STEP TWO: HANG OUT

Psychologists and sociologists have debated for decades whether we *have* selves or *make* them. Some studies seem to demonstrate that each person exhibits a definite personality profile, whether he or she recognizes it or not. From this point of view you're basically an extrovert or an introvert, an optimist or pessimist, mathematically or artistically inclined.

But other studies indicate the opposite. They show that people change, sometimes radically. Where most psychologists used to contend that one's personality is etched in stone during childhood, many now say that profound developmental changes often occur in young adulthood and throughout midlife. "Personality may be more fluid, adaptive, and innovative than is usually thought," Norma Haan, an eminent psychologist at the University of California at Berkeley, concluded shortly before her death in 1988.

In the absence of definitive evidence for either view of the self, my own research shows clearly that to recover from a career crash it's helpful to assume that your self is pliable. Mark Sternberg, thirty-nine, who used to teach college students and currently writes copy for a New York advertising agency, put it well: "In my mind I had to replace that slogan from the army recruitment ads—'Be all you can be'—with a line from the

Mamas and Papas—'Go where you wanna go, do what you wanna do.' That's the attitude I needed to get myself moving in some kind of sensible way."

Denied tenure by the Department of Classics at the university where he had taught for seven years, Mark applied immediately for other teaching posts. "I felt I owed it to myself not to give up this profession just because a bunch of old farts thought I wasn't good enough," he explained. "In fact, I still look at the world through the eyes of a professor of classics. When I watch a cop show on television, I'm not interested in the chase scenes, I'm interested in which Greek tragedy the plot comes from."

But Mark learned quickly the high price he'd have to pay to remain in academia. The few colleges that showed an interest in hiring him were situated out in the sticks. "They all struck me as places where a single man might end up sexually harassing coeds," he said.

For weeks Mark was down in the dumps. Then his older sister called and offered to talk to her husband, the owner of an advertising agency in New York City, about the possibility of hiring Mark in the Creative Department.

"Give yourself a break, come to Manhattan, have some fun," his sister urged.

"Abandon Antigone for Pepsi-Cola commercials?" Mark retorted at first. "No way. My dissertation adviser would turn over in his grave."

But within days he came around to his sister's point of view. Sitting in his living room with a Rand McNally atlas in his lap, trying to locate Greenwood, South Carolina, where he had been invited for a job interview, Mark fixed his attention on an airline commercial on the news program he was half watching on the television. "Shockingly unpersuasive," he remembers thinking.

He canceled the trip to South Carolina and, without resolving to give up teaching permanently—in fact, without resolving anything at all about his long-term plans—found someone to sublet his apartment in Los Angeles on a half-year lease and moved to New York.

Asked at parties what he does for a living, Mark responds that he is open to suggestions. Although the advertisements he has written for his brother-in-law's firm have been well received by clients, Mark refers to the job as "a way station between the career I had planned to have and God-knows-what."

He's the very embodiment of a person in the liminal state, "neither-this-nor-that, here-nor-there," as the anthropologist Victor Turner put it. For now, though, he's enjoying standing on the threshold.

A good case can be made that the most rational thing to do during the liminal stage is nothing at all. Stop work entirely for a while and take a sabbatical.

Of course, many baby boomers don't give themselves sabbaticals for a good reason: they can't afford to. Without a job they'd lose their homes or their children would go hungry. But a surprising number of baby boomers *do* have sufficient savings, inheritance, or spousal income to go for some months without a job. At least half of the people in my study had the means to do so with little or no loss of material comforts.

Yet only a few granted themselves sabbaticals, and those few had to modify their thinking to do so. "The smartest thing I did when I couldn't find work," reports Doug Thompson, "was to expel that little voice in my brain that said I've got to get my career back on track."

After twelve weeks of having doors closed in his face by potential employers, Doug took stock of his situation. None of the jobs he'd applied for appealed to him much. Equally important, his wife was making good money in her own business, and

Josh, their son, was having adjustment troubles at the day-care center, possibly in reaction to tensions at home.

"I said, screw this, I'm going to play Mr. Mom for a while," Doug told me. He took Josh out of day care and cared for him full-time over the next half year until Josh was ready to go to school and Doug himself felt ready to look for a job.

Doug's wife, like many spouses during the second stage of their partners' crashes, experienced a combination of envy, anger, and anxiety. She nearly stopped speaking to Doug, and eventually the two of them had to go to a marriage counselor for help. But in retrospect Doug says of his sabbatical, "Those months were the most worthwhile period in my adult life. The costs we incurred in terms of lost income and strains in our marriage have been repaid many times over by the bond I made with Josh."

STEP THREE: MOVE ON

The liminal period ends when a person determines to settle into a career track again. For Doug Thompson it ended the day he enrolled Josh in preschool and started looking seriously for work. For Seth Gordon, the medical student who used to be a TV director, it began when he enrolled for the premed program at a local college.

But this last stage is less about finding a new place to work than it is about finding a new place *for* work in one's set of priorities.

Until they crash, career is centermost in many baby boomers' lives, the essential source of self-esteem and the activity that eats up nearly all their waking hours. Earlier, I pointed out the historical reasons for this generation's overinvolvement in work. With divorce rates soaring, church attendance sinking, and political heroes dying throughout the 1960s and 1970s, we chose to invest ourselves fully in work, the one institution that remained viable.

Now the tables have turned. Marriage, religion, and politics hold considerable appeal, while work has lost its allure. In the workplace, "empathy is out," as the director of a large search firm told *The Wall Street Journal.* Many of us feel more welcome and secure in our marriages and political and religious organizations than we do at the office.

The critical task during this last stage is to put work in second, third, or even fourth place in one's life, behind family, faith, and politics. But how, in the course of a job search, do post-crash baby boomers actually accomplish that shift?

Some explicitly seek out companies that offer generous child-care or elder-care benefits, or whose politics—judged by their stance on free trade, environmental issues, or the like—is agreeable. Other baby boomers track down those rare employers who pay their managers and executives to get involved in the community—companies like Arco, Xerox, Unum Life Insurance, and the Federal National Mortgage Association (Fannie Mae), which provide technical advisers to minority businesses and mentors to inner-city schools.

Still other baby boomers start their own businesses, become free-lancers or consultants, or go into direct sales in order to have more control over their schedules. They divide up their work and nonwork time according to the needs of their clients, their families, and their community involvements.

Some people go farther still. They find ways to make their living in the service of their religion, politics, or family. Patrick Bristow, thirty-nine, a corporate lawyer, was hired as counsel for his church synod. Steven Ide, forty-six, a dentist, became mayor of his city. Joyce Mayfield, an executive assistant, created a television program about her family. Janine Moran, thirty-six, a former banker, put together a business plan, raised capital, leased a building, hired teachers, and opened the kindergarten where her son is now a student.

Another woman brought her family values to her workplace without ever leaving her old corporation. Grace Kim, thirty-four, a marketing manager with a pharmaceutical firm in New Jersey, established a child-care facility for her company. The way she created this opportunity suggests an important lesson: don't automatically assume that your old employer will reject your new needs and priorities.

Grace, whose enthusiasm for her work had been waning for a few years, crashed while on maternity leave following the birth of her child. She returned to her job because her husband and newborn depended on her income, but she went back bitter, wishing she could stay home. At the office, she withdrew, ate her lunch alone, and treated her staff brusquely.

Eventually Grace's boss came to her office and asked what was wrong. He said he had been called on the carpet several months earlier by a senior director after losing another productive manager, a woman who resigned to take a job closer to her home following the birth of a child. Grace's boss said he didn't want a repeat performance.

Grace spoke honestly with her boss about her waning interest in marketing and her guilt at leaving her baby at a stranger's home every morning. She handed him a stack of clippings she'd been accumulating in her briefcase, articles from *Working Woman, Business Week,* and *The Wall Street Journal* about companies that had become more "family friendly." The articles talked about the reductions in insurance, absenteeism, and turnover costs that result when employees with child-care or elder-care responsibilities have access to company-backed programs.

One of the clippings described how 300 U.S. companies had established "Manager of Work-Family Programs" positions over the past few years. Grace's boss took that article and passed it along to his superiors with the suggestion that Grace might be ideal for such a position.*

When, less than two weeks later, her boss told Grace the company would soon create this new position and that he could "wire" it for her, she perked right up. She didn't even balk at the news that she'd have to go off for a three-week training course, or that the salary for her new position would start nearly 10 percent below her current pay.

"I had only two questions," Grace remembers. "Could my first project be to contract with a local day-care center for special rates and transportation for our employees? And could my daughter be the first to register?" Today she and thirty other employees have their children enrolled at the day-care center Grace lined up.

THE PRIZE

When victors move into their new jobs, is that the happy ending of the story? Having completed all three stages in the comeback process, do they settle down and stay put, never to crash again?

How gratifying it would be to answer "Yes!" and end this book with the promise that everyone who makes the necessary changes after a career crash is inoculated against future upheavals.

But the realities of the work world at the tail end of the twentieth century as well as the demands baby boomers place upon themselves undermine that possibility. With few promotions available inside organizations these days and layoffs and business failures ever-present threats, any sensible person keeps one eye on the exit door.

Add to those realities the baby boom generation's insatiable

*See "Work-family programs get their own managers," *Wall Street Journal,* April 14, 1992, p. B1.

desire to continue growing and exploring until they're too old to sit up and the odds of future crashes appear high. Many baby boomers will escape them, but many others will not.

Victors of previous crashes have no special protection. The difference between them and other baby boomers is that, having prevailed earlier, victors can spot a light at the end of the tunnel.

A poignant moment from one of my interviews keeps popping back into my mind. I was speaking with Barbara Thompson in a Mexican restaurant in Sacramento, California. Three years had passed since Barbara's husband, Doug, got fired and the Thompsons' marriage nearly fell apart; two years since they completed their sessions with a marriage counselor, Doug started selling insurance, and Barbara decided to ease up on her public relations career for a while and have a second child.

Barbara was telling me how close and supportive their marriage has been these past couple of years and how much she enjoys working only part-time while caring for their fourteen-month-old daughter. Then suddenly her smile faded.

I asked what was wrong. "I was just thinking," she responded in a quiet voice, "that this period in our lives is the calm before another storm. Doug and I are settled now, and I'd like to believe it will last, but it can't. He's working on commission; he could burn out at any time.

"Then there's me," Barbara continued. "Once the baby's ready for day care, I'm going to get itchy to return to work full-time. Which means starting my own public relations firm and making no money for a year or two, or taking a job at one of the big firms—long hours, travel, the whole nine yards. Either way, there will be monster adjustments for our entire family."

This was the first time Barbara had acknowledged that there may be more upheavals in the future. The realization stopped her short. "I was so resentful when Doug got fired, it was *such* a

tough time. I don't want us to go through that again," she acknowledged.

For a long minute she said nothing. But then a smile began to
return to her face. "It was tough, but it was worth it," Barbara
declared. "We learned a lot about our marriage and what each
of us wants out of our work and our relationship.

"And don't forget Katie," she added, smiling broadly. "We
have a beautiful little girl we probably never would have had."

She paused again, then said—correctly, I predict—"If it happens again, we'll make it through."

M E T H O D O L O G Y

On average my interviews lasted ninety minutes. The shortest was just over an hour, while the longest was eight hours spread out over five sessions in a two-year period. As a rule, I met with the person in his or her home or office, less often at a restaurant or public park. In a few instances only telephone conversations were possible.

Creating a representative sample of boomers to interview proved to be no easy matter. Neither the government nor private industry publishes lists of people who have lost or left jobs. I did find a few outplacement and career counseling organizations willing to supply names from their client lists for me to contact. But no worthwhile interviews resulted from those efforts. Almost everyone I approached declined the invitation to talk, and those who agreed did not speak very frankly about their experiences.

People are understandably reluctant to talk about intimate details of their lives with a stranger. I soon learned that if I wanted a busy professional to set aside a substantial block of time from his or her schedule and to open up with me, I needed a personal introduction.

Over a period of about a year I developed an extensive referral network throughout the country. Initially I enlisted friends, relatives, colleagues, and former students to identify potential canditates. They gave me names of people from their neighborhoods or workplaces, parents of their children's playmates, fellow members of their health clubs and churches. Career counselors and therapists I interviewed also sometimes recommended that their clients speak with me. In turn, I asked everyone I interviewed for the names of others who'd experienced career crashes.

These strategies resulted in a marvelously diverse sample. Approximately half of my interviewees are women, about one third are single, and the proportion of whites, blacks, Asian-Americans, and Latinos is roughly the same as in the larger population of boomer managers and professionals. Although a large number live in the Northeast and California, midwesterners and southerners are also included in the sample. As for the counselors I interviewed about their clients, these professionals were selected on the basis of their strong reputations within their professions and their special interest in working with baby boomers during career crises.

In short, I employed in this study customary procedures for qualitative sociological interview studies, including "snowball" sampling through referrals, open-ended focused interviews, verbatim transcription of the tape-recorded interviews, and computer-aided coding. In line with norms established by authors such as Robert Coles, Arlie Hochschild, Studs Terkel, and Lillian Rubin, I have edited the segments included here from interview transcripts, rather than reproduce them verbatim. In describing interviewees, I have opted to identify their ethnic background, sexual orientation, or other "special" status only where such is pertinent to the story being told. Readers should not assume that someone is Caucasian and heterosexual who has not been labeled otherwise.

Introduction

Page

14 True, the prestigious Wall Street law firm: Donna K. H. Walters, "Partners under pressure," *Los Angeles Times,* July 7, 1991, pp. D1 and D8.

16 As of mid-1993: Statistics on layoffs and unemployment are from reports from the Bureau of Labor Statistics (BLS). See in particular issues of *Employment and Earnings* from January through May 1993, from which the numbers of unemployed boomer managers and professionals are derived, based on proportions of boomers among managers and professionals. On boomers as prime layoff targets, see Thomas O'Boyle and Carol Hymowitz, "White collar blues," *Wall Street Journal,* October 4, 1990, p. 1. On the fact that large numbers of baby boomers are variously fearful or hopeful about leaving jobs, see Donna Jackson, "Making a choice," *New Woman,* April 1992, pp. 66–70; Jane Ciabattari, "Job market fallout," *Working Woman,* December 1991, pp. 65–67; "A career survival kit," *Business Week,* October 7, 1991, p. 100; Paula Mergenbagen, "Doing the career shuffle," *American Demographics,* volume 13, 1991, pp. 53–54.

16 Career crashes have become a predictable crisis: The DBM survey is discussed in David Kirkpatrick, "The new executive unemployed," *Fortune,* volume 123, 1992, pp. 37–38. According to surveys by another leading outplacement firm, managers now stay in jobs just six or seven years on average, compared to eight or nine years during the

1980s (*Wall Street Journal*, October 20, 1992, p. A1). On generational contrasts, see Paul Leinberger and Bruce Tucker, *The New Individualists*, New York: HarperCollins, 1991.

Chapter 1

BOOMER BUST

21 Initially, my interest was sparked: Darrel A. Regier, Jeffrey Boyd et al., "One-month prevalence of mental disorders in the United States," *Archives of General Psychiatry*, volume 45, 1988, pp. 977–86; Jerome Myers, Myrna Weissman, M. Tischler et al., "Six-month prevalence of psychiatric disorders in three communities: 1980 to 1982," *Archives of General Psychiatry*, volume 41, 1984, pp. 959–67; Lee Robins, J. Helzer, Myrna Weissman et al., "Lifetime prevalence of specific psychiatric disorders in three sites," *Archives of General Psychiatry*, volume 41, 1984, pp. 949–58; Gerald Klerman, Myrna Weissman et al., *Interpersonal Psychotherapy of Depression*, New York: Basic Books, 1984; and see Klerman's comments on these studies in *The Hartford Advocate*, September 25, 1989, p. 17.

21 Until recently, it was the elderly: Barbara J. Felton, "Cohort variations in happiness: Some hypotheses and exploratory analyses," *International Journal of Aging and Human Development*, volume 25, 1987, pp. 27–42; A. Campbell, P. E. Converse, and W. L. Rodgers, *The Quality of American Life*, New York: McGraw-Hill, 1976; and Susan Nolen-Hoeksema, "Life-span views on depression," pp. 203–41 in Paul Baltes et al., *Life Span Development and Behavior*, volume 9, Hillsdale, NJ: Erlbaum, 1988. My assertions are based as well on my own analyses of data from the National Opinion Research Center (NORC) studies.

22 The major focus of baby boomers' discontent: Laura M. Kalb and Larry Hugick, "The American worker: How we feel about our jobs," *The Public Perspective*, volume 1, 1990, pp. 21–22; Michael E. Kagay, "Most jobholders content, poll says," *New York Times*, September 4, 1989, p. 3. Forty-four percent of older workers were satisfied, compared to about 25 percent of workers aged 18 to 49. Other studies, conducted by Vern Bengtson of the University of Southern California and thus far unpublished, also find boomers expressing

considerably less satisfaction with work than their parents.

24 The state of the American economy: Karen Tumulty, "The dead-end kids," *Los Angeles Times Magazine*, October 28, 1990, p. 10; Amanda Bennett, *The Death of Organization Man*, New York: William Morrow, 1990, pp. 183–84.

25 One quarter of college-educated baby boomers: This statistic is drawn from the General Social Survey conducted by the National Opinion Research Corporation in the early 1990s.

25 Far fewer in this age group own their own homes: About 55 percent of Americans aged 25 to 39 own their homes. This number rises to about 70 percent for those baby boomers in their forties. But nearly 80 percent of the generation just older—people in their fifties and sixties—own their own homes. They also were more likely to be property owners when they were the age boomers are now. The number of homeowners between the ages of 25 and 44 dropped by 6 percent between 1980 and 1990. One reason older Americans can afford more or better housing is because their incomes have increased while boomers' have decreased. During 1990, for example, the median income of people 65 or older increased by 1.4 percent, while for those aged 35 to 44 it *decreased* by 2.8 percent. See "Economy's slump cuts a wide swath," *Wall Street Journal*, October 28, 1991, p. B1; Diane Swanbrow, "Baby boomers are falling behind in quest for the dream home," USC *Transcript*, January 20, 1992, pp. 9 and 11; Thomas Exter, "The burden of roof," *American Demographics*, February 1991, p. 6; *American Demographics*, July 1989, p. 12; Kenneth Bacon, "Baby boomers enjoying fruits of rate cuts," *Wall Street Journal*, March 6, 1992, pp. B1 and B10; "Owning a home becomes less common in 80s," *Wall Street Journal*, January 7, 1991.

25 Katy Butler: "The great boomer bust," *Mother Jones*, June 1989, pp. 32–38. A familiar response to complaints such as Butler's is that baby boomers are spoiled. But as Kathleen Newman, an anthropologist at Columbia University notes, baby boomers' expectations actually come from external sources. "One might argue that previous generations managed on the strength of rented apartments and a much-reduced standard of living. This is beside the point. The expectations fueled by the postwar boom period of the 1950s and 1960s have become benchmarks against which descendants measure what is reasonable to expect in life." (Newman, "Uncertain seas," pp. 112–30 in Alan

Wolfe (ed.), *America at Century's End*, Berkeley: University of California Press, 1991, p. 127.)

26 People in previous generations: For perspectives of the Depression generation see Glenn Elder, *Children of the Great Depression*, Chicago: University of Chicago Press, 1974. Data for my analysis on happiness surveys come from the General Social Survey conducted in recent years by the National Opinion Research Center. In the 1988 survey, for example, among those older than baby boomers, considerably more people with college educations and better incomes rate themselves very happy than do their less well off compeers (43 to 31 percent). Among baby boomers, the same number (31 percent) of the less well off describe themselves as very happy, but fewer (36 percent) of the college educated do.

29 People from the parents' generation settled: See Klaus Warner Schaie and Sherry L. Willis, *Adult Development and Aging*, Boston: Little, Brown, 1986, esp. p. 264; Alice S. Rossi, "Life-span theories and women's lives," *Signs*, volume 6, 1980, pp. 4–32.

29 Then came the 1960s and 1970s: Michael C. Kearl and Lisbeth J. Hoag, "The social construction of the midlife crisis," *Sociological Inquiry*, volume 54, 1984, pp. 279–300. See also Dale Dannefer, "Adult development and social theory," *American Sociological Review*, volume 49, 1984, pp. 100–116; and Ski Hunter and Martin Sundel, "Introduction: An examination of key issues regarding midlife," pp. 8–28 in *Midlife Myths*, edited by Ski Hunter and Martin Sundel, Newbury Park, CA: Sage, 1989, p.16.

30 The previous generation's midlife crisis: On baby boomers crashing earlier, see "New ad ploy: Boomers' midlife crisis is chic," *The Boomer Report*, November 15, 1990, p. 4. Coining of the phrase: Elliott Jaques, "Death and the mid-life crisis," *International Journal of Psychoanalysis*, volume 46, 1965, pp. 502–14.

30 time running out: Edmund Sherman, *Meaning in Mid-Life Transitions*, Albany: State University of New York Press, 1987, p. 8; Lawrence S. Wrightsman, *Personality Development in Adulthood*, Newbury Park, CA: Sage, 1988, chapter 5. The book for therapists is Irvin D. Yalom, *Existential Psychotherapy*, New York: Basic Books, 1980. See also Carol C. Nadelson, Derek C. Polonsky, and Mary-Alice Mathews, "Marriage and midlife: The impact of social change," *Journal of Clinical Psychiatry*, volume 40, 1979, pp. 292–98.

30 That may well have been good advice: David A. Chiri-boga, "Mental health at the midpoint," pp. 116–44 in *Midlife Myths*, edited by Hunter and Sundel, cited earlier, p. 138; and Matilda W. Riley, "Women, men, and the lengthening life course," pp. 333–47 in Alice Rossi (ed.), *Gender and the Life Course*, Chicago: Aldine, 1984.

30 Although baby boomers may joke: National Opinion Research Corporation surveys, 1988–91. As above, the comparisons are of the college-educated portions of the samples.

30 Rather than *death* anxiety: The statistics and conclusions are from Carol Hymowitz, "Trading fat paychecks for free time," *Wall Street Journal*, August 5, 1991, p. B1; Nancy Gibbs, "How America has run out of time," *Time*, April 24, 1989, p. 58; John P. Robinson, "Time's up," *American Demographics*, July 1989, pp. 35–36. For an insightful discussion of this topic see Juliet B. Schor, *The Overworked American*, New York: Basic Books, 1991.

31 According to Smelser: Neil J. Smelser, "Issues in the study of work and love," pp. 1–26 in Neil Smelser and Erik Erikson, *Themes of Work and Love in Adulthood*, Cambridge, MA: Harvard University Press, 1980. The graph and discussion about it appear on pages 7–8.

32 Baby boomers lead a much less well ordered existence: Edward Kain, *The Myth of Family Decline*, Lexington, MA: Lexington Books, 1990; "Has the magic gone for good," *The Economist*, August 6, 1988, volume 308, p. 20.

32 The other reason: Walter Kiechel, a writer for *Fortune* magazine, interviewed forty baby boomer managers around the country and reported: "Several times we heard variants on the line, 'I don't much believe in planning for the future,' even from people with several years at the same large company." Walter Kiechel, "The workaholic generation," *Fortune*, April 10, 1989, pp. 50–62.

Chapter 2

DOWNSIZED ACHIEVERS

34 Of the many routes: Perri Capell, "Endangered middle managers," *American Demographics*, January 1992, p. 44; "Labor Letter," *Wall Street Journal*, November 13, 1990, p. 1; Eric R. Greenberg, "The

latest AMA survey on downsizing," *Personnel*, volume 66, 1991, pp. 38–44; and "AMA forecasts continued upswing in downsizings," *HR Focus*, volume 70, January 1993, pp. 1 and 6.

34 Over the past decade: The figures for unemployed managers and professionals are from reports issued by the United States Department of Labor, Bureau of Labor Statistics during the 1980s and early 1990s. The estimate from the outplacement firm and the comments by Drucker are from Amanda Bennett, *The Death of Organization Man*, cited earlier, pp. 15 and 20. The unemployment rate for white-collar managers and professionals remains far lower, however, than for other workers—about one third what sales, technical, and clerical workers suffer, and one fifth the blue-collar unemployment rate. See "A white-collar recession?" *Business Week*, February 4, 1991, p. 20. For an important discussion of the effects of the prolonged recession on working-class Americans, see Lillian Rubin, *Families on the Fault Line*, forthcoming from HarperCollins.

34 managers in their thirties and early forties: O'Boyle and Hymowitz, "White collar blues," cited earlier; Blayne Cutler, "Corporate Victims," *American Demographics*, May 1989, p. 19.

35 A survey of 250 managers: Peter Nulty, "Pushed out at 45—Now what?" *Fortune*, March 2, 1987, p. 29. The situation has been getting worse. A study by a national outplacement company found that it took managers an average of 7.3 months to get new jobs in 1992, compared to 5.3 months in 1989. Gabriella Stern, "White-collar workers face tougher time after layoffs," *Wall Street Journal*, August 24, 1992, p. 1.

36 Because she was single, had some savings: Unsurprisingly, studies find that people with sufficient financial assets to support themselves and their dependents tend to cope with unemployment better than those who are more strapped. David Jacobson, "Models of stress and meanings of unemployment," *Social Science and Medicine*, volume 24, 1987, pp. 13–21.

37 The three negative outcomes: See Angelo J. Kinicki and Janina C. Latack, "Explication of the construct of coping with involuntary job loss," *Journal of Vocational Behavior*, volume 36, 1990, pp. 339–60; and Sandra Perosa and Linda Perosa, "Strategies for counseling midcareer changers," *Journal of Counseling and Development*, volume 65, 1987, pp. 558–62. Other negative repercussions are common as well, but I list the three that are well documented in the literature and consistently reported by the career counselors and therapists I interviewed

throughout the United States. An interview with Hal Steiger, Ph.D., a therapist in Minneapolis, was particularly helpful.

38 Newman has written: Kathleen S. Newman, *Falling from Grace,* New York: Free Press, 1988, p. 77.

39 "institutionally" or "impulsively": Ralph H. Turner, "The real self: From institution to impulse," *American Journal of Sociology,* volume 81, 1976, pp. 989–1016.

39 Which of the two strategies: See Catherine E. Ross and John Mirowsky, "Explaining the social patterns of depression," *Journal of Health and Social Behavior,* volume 30, 1989, pp. 206–19; and David Jacobson, "Models of stress and meanings of unemployment," *Social Science and Medicine,* volume 24, 1987, pp. 13–21.

41 Where does someone find the wherewithal: Julie A. Lopez, "Career women are being helped more, and in new ways, when jobs turn sour," *Wall Street Journal,* July 3, 1992, pp. B1 and B8; O'Boyle and Hymowitz, "White collar blues."

41 Those as resilient as Paula: See Kinicki and Latack, "Explication of the construct of coping," cited earlier, p. 348.

44 For one group: See Craig B. Little, "Technical-professional unemployment: Middle-class adaptability to personal crisis," *Sociological Quarterly,* volume 17, 1976, pp. 262–74; and Kirkpatrick, "The new executive unemployed," cited earlier, pp. 37–38.

45 waves of layoffs: William Power, "Wall Street's numbers add up to bigger layoffs than thought," *Wall Street Journal,* January 14, 1991, p. 1.

46 Crystal-Barkley: Information is from printed materials provided by the Crystal-Barkley Corporation, an interview with Joseph Wiseman, their vice president of corporate programs, and from two articles: Ronald Roel, "Spying a career change," *Newsday,* July 31, 1989, Part III, pp. 1, 6, 7, 11; and Dan Moreau, "Career changers," *Kiplinger's Personal Finance Magazine,* November 1992, pp. 83–86.

47 Richard Bolles's best-seller: Richard Bolles, *What Color Is Your Parachute?* Berkeley, CA: Ten Speed Press, 1992.

Chapter 3

THE CAREER DIVORCE

51 "If the office in which I toil": Peter Ivan Hoffman, "Next, the 'flee decade,' " *New York Times,* February 8, 1990, p. A29.

51 Few of their parents: Seymour Sarason, *Work, Aging and Social Change*, New York: Free Press, 1977 ("one life" is p. 123).

52 Tom Rath: Sloan Wilson, *The Man in the Gray Flannel Suit*, New York, Simon & Schuster, 1955 ("big house" is p. 10; "money is root" is p. 182; "bright young men" is p. 300).

53 When career counselors: This is based upon reports by career counselors I interviewed. The point is made also by Jean Whitney, president of a career counseling organization, in a letter to *The Hartford Advocate*, June 18, 1990, p. 2.

53 Nor do baby boomers share: "our society" quote: Sarason, *Work, Aging and Social Change*, cited earlier, p. 157.

53 Now the pendulum has swung: See Charles R. Scott, "As baby boomers age, fewer couples untie the knot," *Wall Street Journal*, November 7, 1990, pp. B1 and B6.

54 people felt a moral obligation: Although companies commonly claim they use layoffs as a last resort, a survey of 1,204 companies shows otherwise. Only 6 percent tried cutting pay, 9 percent had shortened work weeks, and 14 percent had created job-sharing schemes. "Odds and ends," *Wall Street Journal*, April 14, 1992, p. B1.

54 "By breaking the lifetime-employment contract": Bennett, *The Death of Organization Man*, cited earlier, pp. 208 and 224. Loss of loyalty is only one of several unanticipated personnel costs corporations experience after downsizing. About half of the companies that downsize are sued by former employees, and about two thirds find that they must initiate expensive recruitment programs to replace some of the employees they let go. See "Amputating assets," *U.S. News & World Report*, May 4, 1992, pp. 50–52; and "Managing people," *Wall Street Journal*, January 26, 1993, p. B1.

59 the Richard Bolles book: Bolles, *What Color Is Your Parachute?*, cited earlier.

60 "the new corporate underclass": Joan Rigdon, "Using lateral moves to spur employees," *Wall Street Journal*, May 26, 1992, pp. B1 and B5; Stuart Weiss, "Locked out," *Business Month*, October 1989, pp. 39–43; Christopher Dawson, "Will career plateauing become a bigger problem?" *Personnel Journal*, volume 62, 1983, pp. 78–81; Mary Rowland, "Sidestepping toward success," *New York Times*, January 24, 1993, p. F17.

61 Studies have found that entrepreneurship surges: Anne Murphy, "The start-up of the '90s," *Inc.*, March 1992, p. 34; Bennett, *Death of*

Organization Man, cited earlier, p. 231; Jeanne Saddler, "Start-ups bloom amid economic gloom," *Wall Street Journal,* March 30, 1992, p. B1; Anne Michaud, "Entrepreneur survives crisis to become 'hot,'" *Los Angeles Times,* June 23, 1991, pp. D1 and D18.

61 The entrepreneurial alternative: Joseph Tibbetts, "Avoiding the entrepreneurial trap of the '80s," *Price Waterhouse Review,* volume 31, 1987, pp. 34–43. The figures on small business failures are from telephone conversations with staff at Dun & Bradstreet. Those small businesses that survive are often hurting as well. According to an estimate in *Black Enterprise* (November 1991, p. 25), 43 percent experienced decreases in gross sales recently. See also Michael Selz, "Many ex-executives turn to franchising, often find frustration," *Wall Street Journal,* October 14, 1992, pp. A1 and A6.

65 Nick's drinking masked the depression: For a traditionally masculine guy, a hangover is far easier to endure than the disgrace of feeling defeated. See Catherine K. Riessman and Naomi Gerstel, "Gender differences in idioms of distress after divorce," a paper presented at the meetings of the American Sociological Association, 1989.

66 Carl Jung wrote: *Contributions to Analytical Psychology,* New York: Harcourt, Brace, 1928, p. 193.

Chapter 4

WHEN COUPLES CRASH

73 A kind of waltz of entitlements: This is a contemporary American middle-class version of what anthropologists have noted cross-culturally, namely that "transitions for one individual are often contingent on those of other persons, primarily kin." Gunhild O. Hagestad and Bernice L. Neugarten, "Age and the life course," pp. 35–58 in Robert H. Binstock and E. Shanas (eds.), *Handbook of Aging and the Social Sciences,* New York: Van Nostrand, 1987, p. 37.

78 As recently as the mid-1980s: Arlie Hochschild, *The Second Shift,* New York: Viking, 1989, p. 242.

78 survey of the alumni of Harvard and Stanford: cited in Sarah Hardesty and Nehama Jacobs, *Success and Betrayal,* New York: Franklin Watts, 1986, p. 309.

78 "If you want to know what shunning feels like": Hochschild, *Second Shift*, cited above, p. 244.

78 In upper-income, two-earner families: "Job costs eat up second paychecks," *Wall Street Journal*, April 22, 1992, p. B1. This study also found that for middle-income families, work-related costs consume 56 percent of the second income. See also Shawn Hubler, "Working part-time with full-time planning," *Los Angeles Times*, November 8, 1992, p. D5. The author cites a government study in which 70 percent of U.S. part-time workers said they work part-time not because they cannot find full-time employment, but by choice.

79 "Each suburban wife": Betty Friedan, *The Feminine Mystique*, New York: Dell, 1963, p. 11.

79 "Our fathers and mothers": Kim Triedman, "A Mother's Dilemma," *Ms*, July/August 1989, p. 60. These concerns are not without merit. A recent study found that the income of women who leave the work force drops an average 33 percent when they return. See "Odds and ends," *Wall Street Journal*, February 10, 1992, p. B1.

82 As sociologist Rosanna Hertz: Rosanna Hertz, "Three careers: His, hers, and theirs," pp. 408–21 in Naomi Gerstel and Harriet E. Gross (eds.), *Families and Work*, Philadelphia: Temple University Press, 1987, p. 419. See also Rosanna Hertz, "Financial Affairs," pp. 127–50 in Suzan Lewis, D. Israeli, and H. Hootsmans (eds.), *Dual-Earner Families*, Newbury Hills, CA: Sage, 1992.

Chapter 5

PREMATURE FORECLOSURE

95 Premature foreclosure: the concept is derived from the developmental theories of the psychologist Erik Erikson. See his *Identity: Youth and Crisis*, New York: Norton, 1968 (esp. chapter 4); "The problems of ego identity," *Journal of the American Psychoanalytic Association*, volume 4, 1956, pp. 56–71; and *Childhood and Society*, New York: Norton, 1963.

103 Studies show, too, the considerable impact: The study from which the two-thirds figure comes is Lucy Rose Fischer, "Between mothers and daughters," *Marriage and Family Review*, volume 16, 1991,

pp. 237–48 (and for more information, see Fischer's *Linked Lives*, New York: Harper & Row, 1986). For the other studies, see Kathleen Gerson, *Hard Choices*, Berkeley, CA: University of California Press, 1985, chapter 3; Glen H. Elder, Jr., "Family transitions, cycles, and social change," paper presented at a National Institute of Mental Health Institute on the Family, Santa Fe, New Mexico, June 1987; Diane Sholomskas and Rosalind Axelrod, "The influence of mother-daughter relationships on women's sense of self and current role choices," *Psychology of Women Quarterly*, volume 10, 1986, pp. 171–82; Eileen D. Gambrill and Cheryl Richey, "Criteria used to define and evaluate socially competent behavior among women," *Psychology of Women Quarterly*, volume 10, 1986, pp. 183–96. This body of research indicates that mothers' encouragement was usually to the daughters' good. The premature foreclosure pattern is a negative exception. Even there, in the end the daughters come away with rewarding careers they might not have been equipped to pursue without their mothers' early encouragement, as most of the examples in this chapter suggest.

110 Only in recent times: For now classic studies of the importance of fathers in the career development of professional and managerial women, see Margaret Hennig and Anne Jardim, *The Managerial Woman*, Garden City, NY: Anchor, 1977; and H. Biller, "The father-child relationship," pp. 69–76 in Victor Vaughan and T. B. Brazelton (eds.), *The Family—Can It Be Saved?*, Chicago: Year Book Medical Publishers, 1976.

110 Her father benefits: For an informative historical perspective see L. E. Boose and B. S. Flowers (eds.), *Daughters and Fathers*, Baltimore: Johns Hopkins University Press, 1989, particularly Lynda E. Boose, "The father's house and the daughter in it," pp. 19–74.

113 Noting that this impossible opposition: On fathers feeling free to criticize their career-oriented daughters, see Corinne N. Nydegger and Linda S. Mitteness, "Fathers and their adult sons and daughters," *Marriage and Family Review*, volume 16, 1991, pp. 249–66.

Chapter 6

THE REBEL AT MIDLIFE

115 As adults, their lives differ: Charlotte C. Dunham and Vern

L. Bengtson, "Married with children: Protest and the timing of family life course events," draft paper, School of Gerontology, University of Southern California. See also Jack Whalen and Richard Flacks, *Beyond the Barricades: The Sixties Generation Grows Up*, Philadelphia: Temple University Press, 1989; and Margaret M. Braungart and Richard Braungart, "The effects of the 1960s political generation on former left- and right-wing youth activist leaders," *Social Problems*, volume 38, 1991, pp. 297–315.

116 In point of fact: Whalen and Flacks, *Beyond the Barricades;* and Braungart and Braungart, "The effects of the 1960s," cited above.

117 code of ethics: Whalen and Flacks, *Beyond the Barricades,* p. 13.

123 "The youth revolt": Ibid., p. 14.

123 "freely, expressively, and fully": Ibid., p. 15.

Chapter 7

ANOTHER VIETNAM LEGACY

134 Unknowingly, Kent had been suffering: On PTSD, see *Diagnostic and Statistical Manual of Mental Disorders*, third edition revised, Washington, D.C.: American Psychiatric Association, 1987; and see C. R. Figley (ed.), *Trauma and Its Wake*, New York: Brunner/Mazel, 1985.

134 Contrary to popular myth: Richard A. Kulka and William E. Schlenger et al., *Trauma and the Vietnam War Generation*, New York: Brunner/Mazel, 1990; Ghislaine Boulanger and Charles Kadushin, *The Vietnam Veteran Redefined*, Hillsdale, NJ: Erlbaum, 1986.

134 Although stressful events at work: Leroy Opp, "Normative mid-life concerns among Vietnam veterans with post-traumatic stress disorders," *Journal of Contemporary Psychotherapy*, volume 17, 1987, pp. 174–94; Ghislaine Boulanger and Charles Kadushin et al., "Post-traumatic stress disorder: A valid diagnosis?" pp. 25–35 in Boulanger and Kadushin, *The Vietnam Veteran Redefined*, cited above.

138 Chris quickly returned: See Hillel Glover, "Survival guilt and the Vietnam veteran," *Journal of Nervous and Mental Disease*, volume 172, 1984, pp. 393–97. The term "survivor syndrome" is sometimes used in the business press to describe the reactions of employees who remain in corporations after downsizings. See, for example, Michele B. Morse, "Survivor syndrome," *Success*, September 1987, pp. 58–62; Thomas J.

Murray, "Bitter Survivors," *Business Month*, May 1987, pp. 28–31.

139 In World War II: Joel O. Brende and Erwin Parson, *Vietnam Veterans*, New York: Plenum, 1985, p. 19. Regarding identity development while in Vietnam, see Robert S. Laufer, "War trauma and human development," pp. 33–56 in S. M. Sonnenberg, A. S. Blank, and J. Talboot, *The Trauma of War*, Washington, D.C.: American Psychiatric Press, 1985; Leroy Opp, "Normative mid-life concerns among veterans with post-traumatic stress disorders," *Journal of Contemporary Psychotherapy*, volume 17, 1987, pp. 174–94; Sumner H. Garte, "Still in Vietnam," *Psychotherapy in Private Practice*, volume 3, 1985, pp. 49–53; Norma Wikler, "Hidden injuries of war," pp. 87–113, and John P. Wilson, "Conflicts, stress and growth," pp. 123–65 in C. R. Figley and S. Leventman (eds.), *Strangers at Home*, New York: Praeger, 1980.

144 Unknowingly, Cal administered: John P. Wilson, *Trauma, Transformation, and Healing*, New York: Brunner/Mazel, 1989 (esp. chapter 7); Maja Beckstrom, "Vietnam vets find peace in healing ceremonies," *Utne Reader*, March/April 1991, pp. 34 and 36.

144 Through the rituals: Wilson, *Trauma*, cited above, p. 164

145 When Cal was flown home: Studies of Vietnam veterans find that those who lacked support from their families when they returned home are most prone to delayed PTSD symptoms in later years. See Norman Solkoff, Philip Gray, and Stuart Keill, "Which Vietnam veterans develop post-traumatic stress disorders?" *Journal of Clinical Psychology*, volume 42, 1986, pp. 687–98. On difficulties in relationships with fathers, see Robert Rosen- heck, "Father-son relationships in malignant post-Vietnam stress syndrome," *American Journal of Social Psychiatry*, volume 5, 1985, pp. 19–23.

146 On days when some of his staff: The tendency to drift into combat-mode behavior is common among PTSD victims. Bruce I. Goderez, "The survivor syndrome," *Bulletin of the Menninger Clinic*, volume 51, 1987, pp. 96–113.

Chapter 8

NAKED CAREER COUNSELING

151 Membership in the National Career Development Association:

With research assistance from Susan Aminoff, I counted the listings in telephone books for the metropolitan and major suburban areas of Boston, Chicago, Denver, Los Angeles, New York, Philadelphia, Seattle, and Washington, D.C. The degree of increase varied but was dramatic in almost every case. For example, the Los Angeles directory listed 10 résumé services in 1979 and 58 in 1991; the number of career and vocational guidance firms increased from 16 to 47 during that period. In Seattle, the numbers increased from 13 to 60 for résumé services, and from 16 to 49 for career counseling. The statistic on the National Career Development Association is from a telephone interview with its executive director.

153 They put forward a host of humane-sounding reasons: I heard these comments from several career advisers I interviewed. They appear in the industry literature as well. See, for example, James E. Challenger, "When outplacement is a sham," *Personnel Journal*, volume 68, 1989, pp. 27–30; and Peter Allan, "Tips from the trenches," *Personnel Administrator*, volume 34, 1989, pp. 74–75.

153 Take headhunters: Statistics on headhunters are from Julie A. Lopez, "Executive-search firms find signs of resurgent headhunting," *Wall Street Journal*, May 29, 1992, pp. B1–2; and Ted Rohrlich, "Headhunter's latest worry is joblessness," *Los Angeles Times*, Business Section II, September 16, 1991, pp. 20–21.

153 Yet outplacement counselors: Dyan Machan, "Meet the undertakers," *Forbes*, November 11, 1991, pp. 384–88.

154 *Business Week* magazine rightly suggested: "That's outplacement, not job placement," *Business Week*, October 28, 1991, p. 146. See also Lopez, "Career women are being helped more," cited earlier, p. B1. Lopez cites outplacement counselors who indicate that companies are extending greater outplacement services to women employees for fears of sex-bias lawsuits. For trenchant critiques of the outplacement industry written from within the industry itself, see Challenger, "When outplacement is a sham," cited earlier, and William J. Heery, "Outplacement through specialization," *Personnel Administrator*, volume 34, 1989, pp. 151–55.

155 Likewise, vocational advisers: Summary statements about how conventional career counselors operate are based on interviews with them and with Professor Greg Jackson, coordinator of the career counseling program at California State University at Northridge. Programs like Jackson's provide considerably more sophisticated

training than many career counselors receive before setting up shop. For a listing of about 1,000 career counselors who have master's degrees and other credentials, contact the National Board for Certified Counselors in Greensboro, North Carolina.

155 In the public mind: Studies showing the foibles of tests: Charles C. Healy, "Reforming career appraisals to meet the needs of clients in the 1990s," *The Counseling Psychologist*, volume 18, 1990, pp. 214–26; John G. Carlson and Charles C. Healy, "Testing the test," *Journal of Counseling and Development*, volume 67, 1989, pp. 484–90; Leona E. Tyler, "Testing the test," *Journal of Counseling and Development*, volume 63, 1984, pp. 48–50; Dalton Miller-Jones, "Culture and testing," *American Psychologist*, volume 44, 1989, pp. 360–66; D. Faust and J. Ziskin, "The expert witness in psychology and psychiatry," *Science*, volume 241, 1988, pp. 31–35.

156 Some of the reports that come back: Mary H. McCaulley, "The Myers-Briggs Type Indicator in counseling," in C. Edward Watkins and Vicki L. Campbell (eds.), *Testing in Counseling Practice*, Hillsdale, NJ: Erlbaum, 1990, p. 108.

158 Advisers who subscribe to the fork-in-the-road model: On techniques used by counselors who take a psychologically oriented approach and view crashes from a fork-in-the-road perspective, see Norman C. Gysbers, *Career Counseling*, Englewood Cliffs, NJ: Prentice-Hall, 1987; Elizabeth B. Yost and M. Anne Corbishley, *Career Counseling*, San Francisco: Jossey-Bass, 1987; Thomas M. Skovholt, James Morgan, and H. Negron-Cunningham, "Mental imagery in career counseling and life planning," *Journal of Counseling and Development*, volume 67, 1989, pp. 287–92; G. Edward Watkins, "Using early recollections in career counseling," *The Vocational Guidance Quarterly*, 1984, pp. 271–76.

159 She draws a sharp contrast: Like *foreclosure*, the term *moratorium* is drawn from the work of the psychologist Erik Erikson. See chapter 5 for details.

160 To illustrate how much patience may be required: In relaying information which counselors have shared with me about their clients, I altered the stories to protect confidentiality. In most cases, the counselor and I decided together which details I would change and in which ways. By that means, we came up with a version close or parallel to the actual.

162 In a study of people who changed professions: Hanna Chusid

and Larry Cochran, "Meaning of career change from the perspective of family roles and dramas," *Journal of Counseling Psychology*, volume 36, 1989, pp. 34–41. See also Richard L. Ochberg, "Life stories and the psychosocial construction of careers," *Journal of Personality*, volume 56, 1988, pp. 173–204.

166 "We're the Louds of affirmative action": "An American Family," produced by WNET, aired January 1973.

Chapter 9

BACK TO SCHOOL

168 Asked in a national survey: The survey of adults 21 and older was conducted by Fleishman-Hillard (July 1989).

168 For her doctoral dissertation: Joan Levine, "Taking the Road Not Taken: Career Change for Men and Women in Their Thirties," doctoral dissertation in the Department of Psychology, City University of New York, 1986.

179 "They've got it made": See J. Scott Long, "The origins of sex differences in science," *Social Forces*, volume 68, 1990, pp. 1297–1316; Frances J. Cater and R. C. Norris, "Quality of life of graduate students," paper presented at the meetings of the American Educational Research Association, New Orleans, 1984; Donald Auster, "Mentors and proteges," *Sociological Inquiry*, volume 54, 1984, pp. 142–53.

180 "Mentoring utilizes the parental impulse": Levinson, *Seasons of a Man's Life*, p. 253; and see Cheryl A. Wright and Scott D. Wright, "The role of mentors in the career development of young professionals," *Family Relations*, volume 36, 1987, pp. 204–8.

180 "You naturally make friends": Joan Levine found in her study as well that midlife students form support groups.

181 They really want to be in school: Age also can be an advantage in landing a job after graduation. "When you are 44 and you decide to make a career change, they think you must be pretty committed to doing it," one man noted in an interview with a business magazine. (Dan Moreau, "Career changers," *Kiplinger's Personal Finance Magazine*, November 1992, p. 84.)

• • •

Chapter 10

VICTORS

185 These steps: Arnold van Gennep, *The Rites of Passage*, London: Routledge and Kegan Paul, 1960. See also Victor Turner, "Variations a theme of liminality," in S. Moore and B. Myerhoff (eds.), *Secular Ritual*, Amsterdam, the Netherlands: Van Gorcum, 1977. Thanks to Beverly Farb, whose doctoral dissertation proposal in the Department of Sociology at the University of Southern California led me back to these authors.

189 But other studies indicate the opposite: Norma Haan, "Personality at midlife," chapter 6 in Hunter and Sundel, *Midlife Myths*, cited earlier, p. 152. On the dispute about stability of personality, see also Lawrence Wrightsman, *Personality Development in Adulthood*, Beverly Hills, CA: Sage, 1988, chapter 6; and Ann Swidler, "Love and adulthood in American culture," pp. 120–47 in Neil Smelser and Erik Erikson (eds.), *Themes of Work and Love in Adulthood*, Cambridge, MA: Harvard University Press, 1980.

191 "neither-this-nor-that": Victor Turner, "Variations on a theme of liminality," in Moore and Myerhoff, *Secular Ritual*, cited above, p. 37.

193 Now the tables have turned: *Wall Street Journal*, May 26, 1992, p. 1.

193 The critical task during this last stage: Nella Barkley, a founder of the Crystal-Barkley Corporation (described in chapter 2), argues that career satisfaction is best envisioned as a triangle. At the base is geography—having a job that allows you to live in a place you like. The other two parts are personal values and working conditions. Barkley suggests that after a career crash, many times people need to change only one of the three parts in order to achieve happiness in their work lives. See also Moreau, "Career changers," cited earlier, p. 86.

193 companies like Arco, Xerox, Unum Life Insurance: Diana Tomb, "On leave, with love," *Los Angeles Times*, August 25, 1992, pp. E1 and E8; Charlene M. Solomon, "New partners in business," *Personnel Journal*, April 1991, pp. 57–67; Lois Timnick, "Windows to the world," *Los Angeles Times*, June 11, 1992, pp. J1 and J8.

194 One of the clippings: See "Work-family programs get their own managers," *Wall Street Journal*, April 14, 1992, p. B1.

Methodology

199 For scholarly discussions of the primary research techniques I employed in this study—namely, in-depth interviewing and snowball sampling—and the ways in which excerpts from the transcripts are used, see Bob Blauner, "Problems of editing 'first-person' sociology," *Qualitative Sociology*, volume 10, 1987, pp. 46–64; Steven J. Taylor and Robert Bogdan, *Introduction to Qualitative Research Methods*, New York: Wiley, 1985; and Bruce L. Berg, *Qualitative Research Methods for the Social Sciences*, Boston: Allyn & Bacon, 1989. Regarding the validity of sociological case studies, see J. Clyde Mitchell, "Case and situational analysis," *The Sociological Review*, volume 31, 1983, pp. 187–211.

INDEX

INDEX

A B O U T   T H E   A U T H O R

Barry Glassner is Chair of the Department of Sociology at the University of Southern California. He is the author of *Bodies: Why We Look the Way We Do (and How We Feel About It)*. His articles have appeared in numerous newspapers and magazines. He lives in Los Angeles, California.